Guaranteed Formula for Writing Success

by Everett Ofori
(MBA, Heriot-Watt University, UK)
(MSF - Finance, College for Financial Planning, Colorado, USA)

Guaranteed Formula for Writing Success
Copyright ©2018 by Everett Ofori

ISBN-10   1-894221-12-5
ISBN-13   978-1-894221-11-5

Illustrations: Ahn Soo Kyoung
Cover design: Everett Ofori

Extreme care has been taken to ensure that all information presented in this book is accurate and up to date at the time of publishing. The publisher cannot be held responsible for any errors or omissions. Additionally, neither is any liability assumed for damages resulting from the use of the information contained herein.

All rights reserved. No part of this publication may be reproduced, stored in a retrieval system or transmitted in any form or by any means, electronic, mechanical, photocopying, recording or otherwise without the express written permission of the publisher, except in the case of brief quotations embodied in critical articles and reviews. Printed in the United States of America and the United Kingdom.

CONTACT: Everett Ofori
            Takarazuka University of Art and Design
            Tokyo Campus Building 1F-123MBE
            7-11-1 Nishi Shinjuku
            Shinjuku-ku, Tokyo, Japan
            160-0023

Other books by Everett Ofori

Succeeding From the Margins of Canadian Society:
A Strategic Resource for New Immigrants, Refugees and International Students
Written by Francis Adu-Febiri and Everett Ofori
© 2009 Everett Ofori
ISBN 978-1-926585-27-7

Read Assure: Guaranteed Formula for Reading Success with Phonics
© 2010 Everett Ofori
 ISBN 13   978-1926585833

Guaranteed Formula for Public Speaking Success
©2011 by Everett Ofori
ISBN-13   978-1-926918921

The Changing Japanese Woman: From Yamatonadeshiko to YamatonadeGucci
©2013 by Everett Ofori
ISBN-13   978-1894221047

Prepare for Greatness: How to Make Your Success Inevitable
©2013 by Everett Ofori
ISBN-13   978-0921143000

The Global Student's Companion:
10,001 Timeless Themes and Topics for Dialogue, Discussion,
and Debate Practice
©2015 by Everett Ofori
ISBN-13   978-1894221023

Guaranteed Formula for Effective Business Writing
©2017 by Everett Ofori
ISBN-13   978-1894221108

DEDICATED TO...

ALL THOSE WHO STRIVE FOR CLARITY,

IN WORD AS IN DEED.

Table of contents   Page

Chapter 1	PREP	6
Chapter 2	Quick Introductions	13
Chapter 3	IFONI: Five Types of Examples	19
Chapter 4	Five Ways to Conclude Your Essay	28
Chapter 5	PPF: Past, Present, Future	34
Chapter 6	The WriteBurger	39
Chapter 7	The Two-Handed Mouth	58
Chapter 8	The Narrative Essay	64
Chapter 9	The Definition Essay	87
Chapter 10	The Illustration/Expository Essay	97
Chapter 11	The Descriptive Essay	100
Chapter 12	The Process Essay	121
Chapter 13	The Compare and Contrast Essay	125
Chapter 14	The Classification Essay	131
Chapter 15	The Cause and Effect Essay	134
Chapter 16	The Persuasive Essay	141
Chapter 17	Getting Better as a Writer	144
Chapter 18	101 More Topics for Essay Writing Practice	156

About the Author 159

Chapter 1
PREP

Can the art of good writing be taught? The answer, in short, is yes. Words come more easily to some people than to others, but that does not mean that only a talented few can learn to write well.

In practically every area of human endeavor, even those who have natural talent know the value of training. That is why Michael Jordan and David Beckham, both talented athletes, benefited from having coaches even while at the height of their careers.

Writing is no different. Like sports, there are basic principles that anyone, talented or not, can apply to improve his or her work, although making an earnest effort is also necessary.

Everyone can benefit from learning the art of good writing. Many highly educated people know how to string words together into sentences and paragraphs, but when readers are unable to understand what these writers mean, you cannot just blame the reader. Maybe, the writing is not clear enough. Good writing is clear, coherent and concise.

To write to be understood, it is necessary to prepare before you write and to revise what you have written.

> "ANYONE WHO THINKS CLEARLY SHOULD BE ABLE TO WRITE CLEARLY ABOUT ANY SUBJECT AT ALL."
> - William Zinsser, Writing to Learn

PREP

PREP is a formula for writing. Using PREP, you can write a paragraph that is coherent and concise. Paragraphs, of course, are the basic building blocks of longer compositions.

PREP stands for

- P - Point
- R - Reason
- E - Example(s)
- P - Point

Using PREP will help to make your writing coherent, that is, more unified. Being able to write an effective paragraph is important because, after all, articles, stories, and even books are all made up of a succession of paragraphs.

Let's try using PREP.

Model 1

Let's say your topic is War.

First, make a Point about war. Do you think war is bad? Do you think war is exciting, or perhaps a terrible shame? Express that point.

P – Point: *War is bad.*

Next, give a Reason, or a couple of reasons, why you made that point.

R – Reason: *Why do I say that war is bad? The reason is that war often results in the loss of thousands, if not millions, of lives. War can also contribute to disease and famine.*

To make your writing effective, get in the habit of giving examples. Examples make your point clearer to the reader.

E – Example: *During World War II, for example, many innocent people died. In addition to the thousands of soldiers who lost their lives, millions of civilians were killed. In Germany, during that same war, six million Jews lost their lives. In China, during the Nanjing Massacre, thousands of people were killed.*

End the paragraph by tying everything together. This helps to keep the reader focused on your main idea — the Point you made earlier. When restating the point in your conclusion, it is a good idea to use different words. Variety, as the saying goes, is the soul of pleasure.

P – Point: *War brings misery and death. A world without war is an ideal that I fervently hope for.*

Here's your paragraph on war without the PREP notes.

War

War is bad. Why do I say that war is bad? The reason is that war often results in the loss of thousands, if not millions, of lives. War can also contribute to disease and famine. During World War II, for example, many innocent people died. In addition to the thousands of soldiers who lost their lives, millions of civilians were killed. In Germany, during that same war, six million Jews lost their lives. In China, during the Nanjing Massacre, thousands of people were killed. War brings misery and death. A world without war is an ideal that I truly hope for.

Model 2
Topic: The Japanese educational system

P: *The Japanese educational system is one of the best in the world.*

R: *This is because it has produced some very good results.*

E: *Let's use the example of Japanese companies like Sumitomo, Mitsubishi, Honda and Toyota. These companies are well known around the world because of the quality of their products. In the United States, for example, when people are looking for a good car to buy, they usually choose a Japanese car such as a Honda or a Toyota. In Canada, when people want good electronic products, they usually purchase from Japanese companies such as Sony, Panasonic or JVC.*

P: *Considering the quality of Japanese products, and the fact that these companies became successful by employing workers who were educated in Japan, it is difficult to believe those who claim that the Japanese educational system is bad. In my opinion, it is one of the best in the world.*

Now, not everybody will agree with this opinion, but no one can claim that you were not able to give an answer!

In your example, you could tell a story. Stories are often engaging to read or listen to. When you use a story, try to be specific. What does it mean to be specific? Add details that are realistic and appropriate. A flower is general; a rose is specific. A shop is general; Sogo, Wal-Mart, or Canadian Tire is specific. A car is general; a BMW is specific.

Model 3
Topic: Shopping

P: *Shopping is relaxing...*

R: *...because the shopping environment is designed to create a positive feeling.*

E: *When I go to work I feel stressed, but when I go shopping and see all those colorful clothes — mini-skirts, blouses, jeans, tank tops and swimsuits — I usually feel like I have died and gone to heaven. This is especially true when I have just received my paycheck. Last week, I was feeling really down. I considered quitting my job because my boss is not exactly the kind of person you want to see everyday. When my friend asked me to go with her to the mall, I jumped at the chance. In Shinjuku, at the heart of Tokyo, we made a tour of shops such as Isetan, where we bought two blouses each, then, we went to Mitsukoshi, and later to Gucci and Marui. We caught the last train home, carrying bags and bags of goodies.*

P: *By the time we got home, our purses were empty, but our hearts were full and we felt happy and relaxed.*

Assignment 1

Use PREP to write three paragraphs on the following topics:

1) Computers

2) My hometown

3) Family

Chapter 2
Quick Introductions

You have just received your question as you sit ready to take an English composition test. You are familiar with the topic, and you think you can do a passably good job of writing the essay — if only you can come up with a good introduction! Your mind is blank one moment, and full of facts and ideas the next. You are a little bit confused. Okay, you are very confused, and the clock keeps ticking away.

What if there was a way to write a quick introduction to practically any topic that might appear on the test? Instead of wasting precious minutes worrying about words that will not come, you could start writing your essay in a matter of seconds.

Being able to start writing quickly could also mean being able to review and improve upon what you have written. Going into an exam room confident that you can always write a good introduction is also likely to increase your confidence level.

On the other hand, not being able to start because nothing comes to mind could raise your level of anxiety, which is not a big help when you are taking a high-stakes test.

Here is the formula for Quick Introductions or Quick Intro:

> **Most people think** .
> **For example**, .
> **I think** .

Easy to remember, wouldn't you agree? Let's apply it to an essay topic. Let's say your topic is Pollution. Here is a possible introduction using Quick Intro.

Model 1

> *Most people think pollution is a growing problem in our society. For example, in Hong Kong, some people are unable to breathe properly because of the high level of toxic materials in the air. I think that it's about time the government of Hong Kong got serious and did something about this terrible problem.*

How long would it have taken you to write the above introduction? Not very long, thus, leaving you with more time to complete your essay in the allotted time.

Admittedly, the above introduction is not likely to win you the Nobel Prize for Literature, but it is a start. As you get more practice, you will be able to write more charming introductions without losing precious minutes confused about how to get started.

Let's look at another topic, the Death Penalty.

Model 2

> **Most people think** that the death penalty is important as it helps to preserve order in society. **For instance**, in China and the United States, the government sometimes kills convicted murderers. This is supposed to punish the offenders and discourage others who may be planning to engage in similar serious crimes. **I think** that the death penalty is not necessarily an effective way to deal with violent crime in society because 1) the state sometimes makes mistakes and kills innocent people, 2) when people are about to commit murder they do not think about the consequences to themselves, and 3) if we want to show people that killing is wrong, it is better to lead by example.

The Rule of 3

Did you notice that in Model 2, three reasons are provided following the phrase I think...? This is crucial. Whether in high school, university or the workplace, The Rule of Three works like magic. If you can come up with three points to discuss, you can satisfy almost any reader or examiner.

The three points are important for another reason. You can expand on them later in the body of your essay, providing even more proof that you are a great thinker.

Model 3

> ***Most governments see*** *gambling as a way to boost revenue.* ***For example,*** *in some American states, such as Nevada, and in some countries, or territories such as Macau, gambling provides a significant portion of the government's revenue. Some of this money may go towards helping the poor, the sick and the elderly. Those are good causes, aren't they? However,* ***I think*** *that despite these benefits, gambling should be severely restricted in society because 1) it sometimes leads to broken homes, 2) it provides fertile ground for vices, such as prostitution, and 3) it sends the wrong message to citizens: that hard work is not necessary for success.*

Get in the habit of always racking your brain for three points. Notice that in Model 3, instead of writing "Most people think," we used Most governments see.

It should be obvious that "Most people think..." is a convenient way to begin, but you do not have to always use this opening. Here are a few variations you can use instead of writing "Most people think..." all the time:

- *A general view [among Canadians] is that...*
- *There is a common perception that...*
- *Many people in our society hold the view that...*
- *It is not uncommon for [parents] to think of themselves as...*
- *It is a widely held view among [schoolchildren] that...*

Most People's View versus My View

You may find yourself using "Most people think…" in those cases where your views differ from the common opinion. In other words, even though "Most people" think a certain way, after careful thought, you may want to express a different view.

Here is an illustration that can help you understand your position as a writer and commentator: It is dark. In the distance somebody sees what appears to be a human figure, dancing in the moonlight. Everybody who passes by agrees that the figure looks like a ghost; after all, exactly a year ago, Ping Ping Tang died in that very spot. No one is willing to go closer to find out the truth, but people keep spreading the rumor that the dancing figure is a ghost.

Now, you are a student of science, and fearless.. From your window, you use a powerful pair of night vision binoculars to zoom in on the image. It looks like a dancing ghost all right, but it seems to be supported by a rod. There are also various tattered cloths hanging around the stick. You realize that the so-called ghost is located smack in the middle of Old Man Tomohiro's garden.

You conclude that it is a scarecrow. You prepare to share this information with the people around you.

> *Most people passing through Dumont Village in the evening conclude that the dancing figure on Littleton Road is a ghost. For example, the figure does not talk back when people shout greetings to it, and there are times when it is not visible, almost as if the ghost gets tired of being stared at. I think that the figure is a scarecrow because 1) it is shaped like a scarecrow, 2) it is located in Old Man Tomohiro's garden, and 3) the main source of the ghost rumors is Old Man Tomohiro himself!*

You have shown that your thinking is different from that of "most people," and you are able to back up your thinking with clear facts and figures. There is an element of opposition or contrast in many essay introductions. This is often signaled by the use of the words "although" or "but."

"Although" the figure looks like a ghost, my research indicates that it is a scarecrow. Here are my reasons: 1) Point A, 2) Point B, and 3) Point C.

Assignment 2

1) Write a Quick Intro to the following topic: **Tourism in my city**

2) Write a Quick Intro to the following topic: **Volunteering**

3. Use PREP to write a passage on the following topic: **Leadership**

Chapter 3
IFONI:
Five Types of Examples

Examples and illustrations are the lifeblood of any composition or essay. If the examples are well chosen, they leave the reader with a feeling of satisfaction as he or she leaves with a deeper understanding of the point the writer wants to make.

Sometimes, however, getting appropriate examples can be a problem. You just don't know where to start.

Let's look at five example types that are easy to remember. Also, note that the examples need not always be based on facts. It is possible to provide an imaginary example, but of course, in such a situation, you simply let the reader know that the example is not factual.

IFONI

I – Individual	Me, Mr. Fumito, Miss Tracy Wong, etc.
F – Family	My own family, The Jacksons, The Tanakas, etc.
O – Organization	A company, a school, a church, a hospital, the fire service, etc.
N – Nation/ Government	Canada, Japan, China, Chile, Tanzania, etc.
I – International	United Nations, World Trade Organization, any form of international or interregional cooperative

Let's do a Quick Introduction plus Body paragraphs based on the subject of FRIENDSHIP.

These have been put into individual boxes just for illustration purposes: After the introduction, we draw examples for the paragraphs from IFONI.

Topic: Friendship

Introduction

> **Most people believe** *that friendship is important.* **For instance,** *people with friends can feel relaxed from day to day because, when they are in trouble, they know they can call on someone they can rely on.* **I think** *that friendship gives us a strong reason to live because 1) friends affirm our worth, 2) friends provide us with numerous opportunities to relax and to have fun, and 3) friends can help us enjoy the feeling of peace and security.*

Paragraph 2
friends affirm our worth

INDIVIDUAL

This example focuses on an individual, Fumito, and how his self-worth was affirmed by a true friend, Wing-Nan.

> *Friends can make us feel special. Even when we are not feeling very good about ourselves we can count on good friends to remind us that we are wonderful people. A young boy, Fumito, recently moved to a new school where he could not make any friends. The children in the school came from very wealthy families and did not think that Fumito's family measured up to their expectations of wealth. For a few weeks Fumito felt sorry for himself and wished that his family had more money.*
>
> *Meanwhile, everyday after school he chatted on the Internet with one of his friends, Wing-Nan, from his previous school. Wing-Nan constantly talked to Fumito about how much people missed him from his old school. Wing-Nan asked permission to pass on Fumito's email address to some of their mutual acquaintances.*
>
> *Gradually, it dawned on Fumito that gaining the acceptance of the children in the new school was not the most important thing he could do. He already had friends who valued him and so he decided to put more effort into maintaining the relationships with his old friends and acquaintances. The friends from his previous school valued him for who he was; Fumito did not see any reason to seek the company and approval of people who could not see any value in him.*

Paragraph 3

Friends provide us with numerous opportunities to relax and to have fun – here the example is drawn from FAMILY. It's a bit tricky turning family members into friends but it's not all that unusual. Tiger Woods, the golf great, has said more than once that his late father was his best friend!

Friends can bring fun and joy into our lives. For Charlene, friendship meant family. She felt most comfortable with people in her family who were never short of ways to bring a smile to her lips. This included members of her large extended family – cousins, uncles, aunts, and various other relatives. Charlene's life was a whirlwind of activity. Whenever her birthday rolled around on February 7th, her family made it special for her.

Charlene's birthday, however, was only one of numerous birthdays and occasions that the family celebrated. In between eating birthday cakes, there were picnics to attend, beaches to visit with the family, and exchange of visits, all of which provided perfect opportunities for various family members to show off their cooking skills. Charlene admits that she does not have many friends outside her family but she insists that anyone lucky like her to have such a loving family would not miss not having any close friends; she is having the time of her life.

Paragraph 4
INTERNATIONAL

Friends can help us enjoy the feeling of peace and security.

For nations, having the right friends can make a big difference in terms of security. Smaller nations are often in greater need of aligning themselves with more powerful nations so that they can enjoy much needed protection in a world of never-ending threats. Many countries in Eastern Europe, for example, have become a part of the European Union because they know that this can mean greater economic prosperity for their countries. More than that, however, being a part of the European "club" provides a guarantee that in the case of an attack, other members will provide the necessary backing. In fact, some of the former aggressors in Europe are very much a part of the European Union and can use their strength, not to bully their smaller cousins, but to provide necessary protection for all who fall within this increasingly important regional grouping.

Now, let's focus on the topic of Pollution, which we used in Chapter 2 (Model 1) and see how we can expand upon it by drawing examples from IFONI.

Paragraph 1
Introduction

> ***Most people think*** *pollution is a growing problem in our society.* ***For example****, in Hong Kong, some people are unable to breathe properly because of the high level of toxic materials in the air. Sadly,* ***I think*** *the government is unlikely to do anything about it because 1) economic considerations are very important to the HK government, 2) Hong Kongers have been too passive regarding pollution, and 3) regional cooperation is essential to dealing with the problem.*

Paragraph 2
Economic considerations are very important to the HK government.
(NATION)

> *The Hong Kong government appears to measure success mostly in terms of the economy. When businesses are doing well and the coffers of Hong Kong are filled, the government of Hong Kong lays claim to the success. With money available, the government is able to take care of its obligations, including the provision of welfare for the poor. Protecting the source of Hong Kong's wealth, from the government's point of view, includes ensuring that businesses can keep on producing. The result is that the government is lax in enforcing anti-pollution measures. This even extends to the issue of pollution from cars on Hong Kong roads.*

Whereas some countries such as Canada have strict tests for cars on their roads, Hong Kong does not appear to put enough pressure on the business community make the environment seem like a priority. This may be because the government is afraid that its own revenues will be seriously affected if punishes businesses that hurt the environment.

Paragraph 3
Hong Kongers have been too passive regarding the issue of pollution.
(INDIVIDUALS)

Individual Hong Kongers have, from time to time, banded together to make their power felt. For example, after the 2004 tsunami that devastated parts of Indonesia, India, and Sri Lanka, Hong Kongers came in as the highest donors per capita. This goes to show how much Hong Kongers can accomplish when they come together for the benefit of a good cause. But while Hong Kongers are willing to open their purses to the suffering, they have not been willing to speak out loudly about the pollution issue. Occasionally, someone writes about the need for the government to take action, but it seems as though Hong Kongers, as individuals, have been all too willing to accept pollution as a part of life in Hong Kong. This, however, need not be. If people were to pressure the government, it is likely that the government would eventually take steps to reduce pollution. Hong Kongers need to understand that the power to change the territory is in their hands.

Paragraph 4
(INTERNATIONAL)

A regional response may be necesary to deal with the widespread pollution in the area.

> *Even if the Hong Kong government got tough on polluters in the territory, this would probably have minimal impact. The reason is that much of the pollution in Hong Kong comes from outside the territory. As such, the Hong Kong government would have to work with their colleagues in Mainland China if they want to make any progress in dealing with pollution. In recent years, there have been indications that the governments of the two territories are willing to work together on this issue.*
>
> *Unfortunately, on both sides of the border, economic considerations seem to dominate. In fact, countries in Asia need to begin thinking about balancing economic progress with environmental protection in order to guarantee that the base of prosperity is not irreparably damaged.*

Paragraph 5
Conclusion

Note

You have probably noticed that the conclusion sections have been left blank. In the next lesson, we will take a close look at Conclusions.

Assignment 3

1. Your topic is **Success**.

Write an introduction that ends with three points you want to make about success. For each of the three points, indicate what kind of example (from IFONI), that you plan to use and write down some brief points about the example in question.

Quick Introduction:

2. Use PREP to write on the following topic: The elderly in society

Chapter 4
Five Ways to Conclude Your Essay

The conclusion of an essay can be one of the most memorable parts, providing of course, that the writer has put in great care to make it so. Also, remember that if you are a student, your instructor is likely to grade your paper after reading the conclusion so if that part is good, it can influence what kind of mark or grade you get. Of course, it would not hurt to write an essay that is good from beginning to end, with the conclusion merely being the frosting on the cake.

Here are five ways to conclude your essay. Depending on your topic, one type of conclusion may be more suitable than another so put some thought into how you craft your conclusions.

1. Straight summary
In the body of the essay, you have discussed in detail the reasons for your choice and supported them with stories and examples. In the conclusion, you summarize the points you have made. Try to express your points in brief, preferably using words other than what you had used before.

Here below is a possible conclusion using the summary method. (Imagine that these points have already been discussed)

Topic: Choice between buying a house and buying a business

If I were older and had some experience of running a business, I would have considered buying a business. But, at my age, buying a house seems more reasonable. It is likely that house prices would appreciate, which means that I can sell the house in the future and use the money to pursue my dreams. At this point, buying a house would allow my family to live in more spacious surroundings and to move out of our small apartment. And finally, I am still enjoying the life of a student, which alternates between studying and enjoying carefree days. Buying a house would allow me to continue this lifestyle, whereas, buying a business will put a responsibility on my head for which I am not fully prepared.

2. Point to Ponder: Question

There are times when we do not want to force our opinions on others. We want them to think for themselves after we have presented our reasons for choosing a particular course. A question is often a good way to stimulate our reader to think carefully about our message. Ending your essay with a question, therefore, could leave the issue ringing in the mind of the reader for some time. Here below is an example.

Topic: Studying alone versus studying with a group

Studying with a group makes so much sense because members of the group can help one another. Often, students have different strengths, with some excelling in mathematics and the sciences while their counterparts may be so much better in the arts. Such an exchange can help boost the results of all the students in a study group while those studying alone suffer in silence when confronted with a problem they cannot solve. Students studying in a group can take the kind of refreshing breaks that we all need when focusing intently on a subject for long periods; they can chat at strategic intervals with study mates. Though there are numerous advantages to studying in a group, would you want to study with group members who are more interested in gossiping and chatting for long periods even as the examination date approaches?

3. Shocking statement

Readers are bombarded all day and night by facts, alternative facts, and opinions. People have become accustomed to hearing all kinds of strange stories, making it rather difficult to catch and hold the reader's attention. A truly shocking statement, however, can do the trick. If you can cite the source of the shocking statement, all the better.

Topic: **Cigarette Smoking**

There are many reasons people smoke, some for the so-called pleasure they get from the habit, others because it supposedly relaxes them, and still others because it apparently makes them look cool. Regardless of the reasons for which people decide to smoke, it is important for them to realize that for every breath of smoke they take they are hastening their trip to the grave. After all, every year, 400,000 men and women, almost half a million, die in the United States as a result of smoking.

4. Lessons learned

You can organize your conclusion in terms of major lessons learned. Of course, a good reader is likely to have understood those points already. It does not hurt, however, to remind the reader of the key lessons in your conclusion.

Topic: **Public Speaking**

Participating in the public speaking competition was a scary experience, but a good one. Even though my knees shook violently while I was on the stage, and I seemed to blank out every few minutes, I managed to pull through with my speech; looking at the sea of faces before me and receiving periodic bursts of applause made my heart quicken in excitement. It was a good thing my heart did not give out from all the joy I felt after the speech was over. It was revealing to me that something so scary could be at the same time so exhilarating. If I have the chance to speak in public again I surely will go for it. I know that I will get the jitters but I also know that I will feel a sense of power, excitement, and accomplishment when I am on the podium.

5. A Call to Action

There are times when we feel so strongly about an issue and desire so much to see something done about it. In such a case, a call for action seems the best conclusion. You signal to the reader that the issue is urgent and that the reader's immediate assistance can make a difference.

Topic: **Homelessness in Canada**

First time visitors to Canada are often shocked to find that there are many homeless people on the streets. This flies in the face of the image that many people around the world have of Canada. For many, Canada is not only a beautiful place but also a place where the government really cares about the people. It is true that some of the homeless people abuse drugs or have mental health issues but there are also many homeless people for whom the problem is simply low wages, making it difficult for them to afford the high rents demanded by landlords.

The government of Canada should not wait until many more homeless people freeze to death before building shelters to take care of this problem; the government should not wait till a million people are on the streets before building more affordable homes. The government should make it a priority to solve the homelessness problem. There has been enough talk about the homeless issue. It's now time to build more shelters, provide more affordable housing, and make all Canadians feel at home in this wonderful land.

Now we have covered all the major parts of an essay: introduction, body comprising three paragraphs, and conclusion. This brings us to the 5-paragraph essay. From now on, all assignments will follow the 5-paragraph essay format though we will make refinements along the way.

Assignment 4

Write a 5-paragraph essay on the following topic complete with examples and a thoughtful conclusion:

Should pets be treated as if they were members of the family?

Chapter 5
PPF: Past, Present, Future

PPF is an organizing principle that can be useful in filling the body of an essay through the logical development of an issue, especially one that involves growth or change over time.

In much briefer form, PPF can also work well for a conclusion.

First, let's see how we can use PPF to organize our composition.

Let's say, our topic is Hong Kong Women.

- P: **In the past**, women in HK did not enjoy equality with men.
- P: The social climate **at present** gives women in Hong Kong equal opportunity.
- F: **The future** holds even greater prospects for women in HK.

Paragraph 1: Introduction

****Most people think*** *that Hong Kong women are strong and achievement-oriented.* ***For example,*** *there are many senior female government officials in the territory. A number of Hong Kong businesswomen have also made their mark, showing that they are as smart as their male counterparts. In fact, Hong Kong women in the past did not enjoy equality with men, but the social climate* ***now*** *gives women in Hong Kong equal opportunity, and there are signs that* ***the future*** *holds even greater prospects for them in Hong Kong, Asia's World City.*

Note:
The three points, highlighted above, will now be developed in three separate paragraphs. For a 5-paragraph essay, you have something along the following lines:

> Introduction
> Paragraph 2 – PAST
> Paragraph 3 – PRESENT
> Paragraph 4 – FUTURE
> Conclusion

The first sentence of each of the paragraphs, 2, 3, and 4, is known as the TOPIC SENTENCE. It gives the reader an idea of what to expect. It captures the main point of that paragraph in one sentence.

In fact, if you have remembered to provide three points in your thesis statement, then each of the three points becomes a topic sentence. Your first point becomes the topic sentence for Paragraph 2; your second point becomes a topic sentence for Paragraph 3; and finally, your third point becomes a topic sentence for Paragraph 4.

Avoid using the exact words in the introduction in your topic sentence; make sure that the points made in the thesis statement are presented clearly using other words. By using synonyms, you introduce a bit of variety into your writing and signal to the reader that you are a versatile writer, not one stuck on using the same words or phrases over and over and over again.

The topic sentences have been bolded in each of the three paragraphs on the next couple of pages:

Paragraph 2: Past

In the past, women were prisoners to the demands of tradition. *It was not uncommon for Hong Kong women to stay at home and take care of their children and husbands. While some women may have found satisfaction in this traditional role, there were not many opportunities for women who wanted to have more knowledge or for those who sought to contribute to society as lawyers, politicians, or doctors. Women cooked, cleaned, and cared for those in the household and had to content themselves with making the home their principal, or perhaps, only place of control.*

Paragraph 3: Present

Today, *women in Hong Kong have become part of practically every sphere of social activity, including those that used to be considered the domain of men. Thus, it is possible to find architects, engineers, doctors, lawyers, and politicians who are respected just as much as their male counterparts. The government of Hong Kong has no doubt played a role in this by providing equal access to education for both boys and girls. Today, women can dream big and not have to worry that traditions will keep them from achieving their cherished dreams.*

Paragraph 4: Future

The future *for young girls growing up in Hong Kong and for women in general looks fairly bright. As more and more women get the opportunity to serve in positions of leadership they inspire little girls to strive harder to make their own dreams a reality. Anson Chan Fang-on Sang, former Chief Secretary of Mr Tung Chee Hwa, Hong Kong's first Chief Executive after the handover of Hong Kong to China in 1997, is only one of many prominent women in Hong Kong whose contributions make Hong Kongers proud.*

Paragraph 5: PPF for Conclusion

While in the past *the status of women in HK was low****, at present,*** *women do not have to be stuck at home. Women fill positions of influence in many fields.* ***In the near future****, it will not be surprising to find that the person in the Chief Executive's office is not in a bowtie but rather one wearing a crisp, pink ribbon in her hair! What a bright day it would be not only for women but for all who care about equality and fairness in society.*

Assignment 5

Using PPF write about Economic and Social Change in Japan, China, or your own country or territory. (You can discuss issues such as farming, factory work, and limited opportunities in the past, the incredible boom in manufacturing, export, and entrepreneurship in recent years, and what the future holds, both for those who are taking advantage of these opportunities and those who might be missing out because of lack of education or lack of connections).

Alternatively, you can choose any other topic that you think will allow you to reflect on the past, the present, and the future.

Chapter 6
The WriteBurger

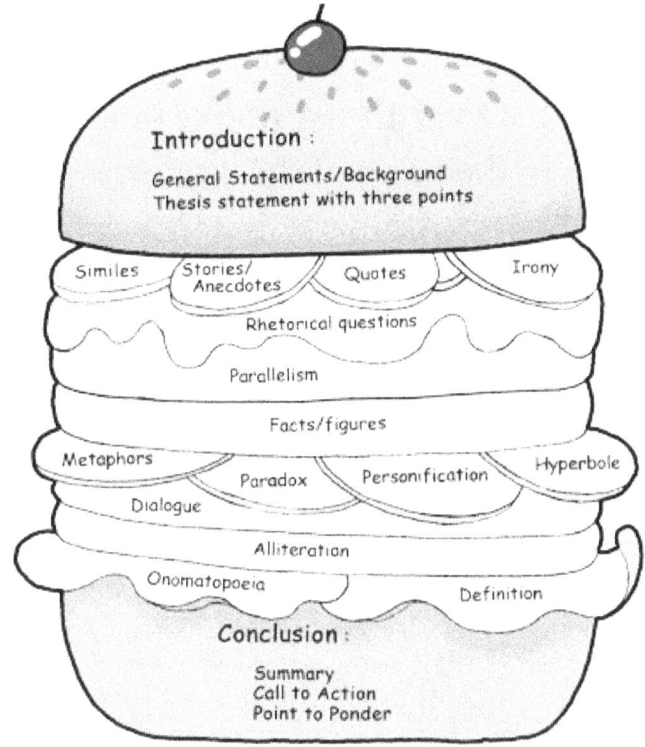

When you order a burger, whether a cheeseburger, a Big Mac or a Fish burger, you take it for granted that you will get two halves of a bun – the top bun and the bottom bun. You cannot imagine getting a burger without one of the two. Likewise, in a composition, you need both the top bun – the introduction – and the bottom bun – the conclusion.

But imagine ordering a burger and getting only the top bun and the bottom bun without anything in between. You might get angry. Unthinkable! After all, what makes a burger such a delight to eat is not just the buns that you get, but what you get between the buns – the cheese, lettuce, onions, pickles, mayonnaise, and whatever else you might fancy.

To make your composition interesting, you also need to put in some yummy "ingredients" between the introduction and the conclusion. You understand that you need to provide examples, but how you present these examples can make all the difference. Let's take the tasty treats one by one and examine them.

Similes:

We create similes when we use the word like or as to compare two things. This creates an image in the mind of the reader.

>For example,
>- *My grandfather is like a bull; he can carry five men on his back.*

>- *My little sister is like a hibiscus, so pretty and delicate.*

There was about three inches of snow on the ground, and it was still coming down like a madman.

  (J.D. Salinger, A Catcher in the Rye)

Exercise: Write 5 of your own similes on various subjects

1. _____

2. _____

3. _____

4. _____

5. _____

Metaphor:

A metaphor is very similar to a simile. The main difference is that instead of using "like" we use is, in effect, creating an equation.

- *My grandfather is a bull; he can carry five men on his back.*

That is, "My grandfather" = bull

- *Jesus said, "You are the salt of the earth."*

That is, "You" = the salt of the earth

- *Peter, a bear of a man, kicked in the door and pulled out his wife from the raging fire.*

That is, Peter = bear-like man

Exercise: Write 5 of your own metaphors on various subjects

1. _____

2. _____

3. _____

4. _____

5. _____

Hyperbole:

Hyperbole is exaggeration – to the extreme.

- *My best friend is so short he can kiss an ant!*

- *Peter is so tall he can sit on the tallest building in the world and still have his feet firmly on the ground.*

- *Oh, did I tell you? Peter's younger brother is so tall he can scratch the sky.*

- *...he had his goddamn knees on my chest, and he weighed about a ton.*

    (J.D. Salinger; A Catcher in the Rye)

Exercise: Write 5 of your own hyperboles on various subjects

1. _____

2. _____

3. _____

4. _____

5. _____

Irony:

We use irony when we say the opposite of what we mean. This makes your conversation or writing more interesting. As Merriam Webster explains, irony is "the use of words that mean the opposite of what you really think especially in order to be funny" or "a situation that is strange or funny because things happen in a way that seems to be the opposite of what you expect."

For example:

- *That Naomi Campbell. Isn't she ugly!*

Of course, most people believe Naomi Campbell is beautiful so the speaker does not really mean she is ugly. Or, it's raining heavily outside; you take one look at the wet streets and declare:

- *What fine weather we are having today!*

Exercise: Write 5 of your own examples of irony on various subjects.

1. _____

2. _____

3. _____

4. _____

5. _____

Parallelism:

Parallelism involves using the same grammatical pattern several times – three times seems to give the greatest effect.

- *Let us never give up.*
- *Let us never surrender.*
- *Let us never yield.*

Exercise: Write 2 examples of parallelism below.

1. _____

   _____

2. _____

   _____

Paradox:

On first hearing a paradox we think the writer or speaker has made a mistake because the ideas seem to be contradicting each other, but when we think a bit more deeply we realize that there is some truth in the statement even though it seems to contradict common sense.

- *When I asked her if she loved her husband she did not respond. Her silence spoke loudly about how she truly felt about him.*

- *She began to listen when I stopped talking.*

- *When I asked her if she wanted to participate in the game her silence was deafening.*

Exercise: Write 2 of your own examples of paradox below.

1. _____

_____

2. _____

_____

Facts and figures:
- *Every year, 400,000 Americans die from prolonged use of cigarettes.*

Exercise: Write 5 of your own sentences that include facts and figures.

1. _____

2. _____

3. _____

4. _____

5. _____

Stories and anecdotes:

Stories and anecdotes (defined by Merriam Webster's Dictionary as a "short narrative of an interesting, amusing, or biographical incident"), can help us expand upon our points. They can help the writer clarify, for example, abstract ideas such as love, honesty, friendship, or cruelty.

> *There is an old story about two brothers in ancient Greece whose city was about to be destroyed by the ruler of a neighboring city. Ten years earlier the two brothers had saved the invading king's life, and so, the king wanted to do a good turn for the brothers. He summoned the two brothers to the city gate and told them that they could get out of the city with anything they wanted but whatever possessions they took had to be carried on their person. They couldn't carry these on horses or in carts. The two brothers duly went back to the city and returned shortly thereafter. One was carrying their mother; the other, their father.*

Exercise: Share an anecdote on a subject of your own choosing

Personification:

Personification is when we give something that is not human the characteristics of human beings.

> For example:
> • *As John set foot in the woods, all the trees bowed to him, giving him the confidence he needed to accomplish the task he had set before him.*

Exercise: Write 3 examples of personification below.

1. _____

_____

2. _____

_____

3. _____

_____

Idioms:

Idioms are special expressions whose meanings cannot be understood from the words making up the idiom. For example,

> • *Old Petro kicked the bucket yesterday.*

You know the meaning of "kick" and "bucket" but the overall meaning is not that Old Petro used his foot to hit a bucket. The meaning of "kick the bucket" as an idiom, is "to die."

> *"Old Petro kicked the bucket yesterday," therefore, means: Old Petro died yesterday.*

There are hundreds of idioms that pose problems for non-native speakers of English. The good news is that most languages have idioms and other metaphorical expressions, so it is not difficult to get people to understand that, not everything they read in English should be taken literally.
In China, for example, people talk about government workers having an "iron rice bowl." This means that their jobs are secure and they do not have to worry about losing their livelihood.

When you write an essay and you use a number of appropriate idioms you signal to the reader that you are more than just a beginning student of English. You signal that you are writing at the level of the native speaker or at least you are very close.

The Internet has several sites that explain the meaning of English idioms. Do a search and once you find a site that is useful, do visit often.

Alternatively, you can get a book of English idioms with exercises. If you read a lot you will come across many idioms, some of which you will understand because of the context in which it is used. Others will send you running to the Internet or a book of idioms because they are not so easy to understand.

Such top-notch magazines as Newsweek, Time, or The Economist, frequently use idioms, meaning that you will always be playing catch-up if you do not have a full understanding of the wide range of idioms currently in use.

Exercise: Find 5 idioms and use each to make a senteence.

1. _____

_____

2. _____

_____

3. _____

_____

4. _____

_____

5. _____

_____

Onomatopoeia:

These refer to words that are coined from sounds around us.

- *The hissing of snakes.*

- *She fell with a thud.*

- *The chickens clucked all day long.*

As with idioms there are many sites on the Internet that are devoted to sharing information about onomatopoeic words. Get acquainted with such sites.

Exercise: Find four examples of onomatopoeia. Use each in a sentence below.

1. _____

_____

2. _____

_____

3. _____

_____

4. _____

_____

Alliteration:

When you have a repetition of (usually initial) consonant sounds you have alliteration. (In this case, s, s, s, s)

Here is one of the most famous alliterations in English:

> *Peter Piper picked a peck of pickled pepper; a peck of pickled pepper Peter Piper picked. If Peter Piper picked a peck of pickled pepper where is the peck of pickled pepper Peter Piper picked?*

The kind of alliteration you might use in an essay need not be too long. If you have three or four words with similar consonant sounds, that is good enough. Sometimes, alliteration will come to you easily; other times, you might have to make a conscious effort to come up with a suitable set.

Once you are aware of the possibilities of using alliteration to enhance your writing, you can experiment. You will realize that with practice and some effort, it will not be difficult to come up with your own to fit a particular situation. Also, when you read, pay attention to how other writers present alliterations and other figures of speech.

Exercise: Write 3 examples of alliteration below.

1. _____

2. _____

3. _____

Some figures of speech

1. When he saw my grandmother's picture on the altar, again his tears fell like rain. [Kitchen, Yoshimoto Banana – simile]

2. After a while we would all just laugh, remembering Madeleine going down the road in her red jacket, with her legs like scissors. [Alice Munro – simile]

3. Time will seem to have added wings to his heels as well as his shoulders. [Benjamin Franklin - imagery]

4. *The space that cannot be filled, no matter how cheerfully a child and an old person are living together – the deathly silence that, panting in a corner of the room, pushes its way in like a shudder.*
    [Yoshimoto Banana – personification/simile]

5. *...her body hissed and trembled above me like a monument about to explode.*
    [Alice Munro – simile]

6. *She's a tiger.* [metaphor]

7.. *When my grandmother died, time died too.*
    [Yoshimoto Banana – personification]

8. Their faces shone like buddhas when they smiled.
    [Yoshimoto Banana – simile]

9. There is fire in the minds of people who have been oppressed for a long time. [metaphor]

Assignment 6

Should animals be confined in zoos for the pleasure of human beings?

Being a good writer means having to make judgments. For assignment number 6 exercise your judgment. Choose which technique/formula would best allow you to discuss the topic in five paragraphs. Please remember to include some figures of speech such as similes, metaphors, hyperbole, etc.

Also, please organize your essay according to the classic 5-paragraph essay format. This means thinking through your thesis statement and coming up with three points, which you expand in the three middle paragraphs.

(The template on the next page regarding the 5-paragraph essay format can be helpful)

Classic 5-paragraph essay
Video games : good or bad?

- Introduction — General statements (3-5 sentences)

  Thesis statement (1 sentence with 3 points ; show contrast by using "although" or "but")

  Most people think video games are a waste of time.................

  Although video games can waste time they can also help children to relax(1), develop hand-eye coordination(2), and strengthen(3) friendship bonds.

- Paragraph 1 : Start topic sentence with point 1

  (1) Playing video games can be very relaxing.
  ....
  [Explain with examples ; tell a story, e.g., Louis eases stress after school by playing video games]

- Paragraph 2 : Start topic sentence with point 2

  (2) Frequently playing video games can help develop hand-eye coordination..........
  [Give examples - surgeons who play video games do better at surgery]

- Paragraph 3 : Start topic sentence with point 3

  (3) Young people who play the same video games always have something to talk about
  [Friends play together, shop for new games, discuss games they have played.]

- Conclusion :

  [Choose a fitting conclusion !]

Chapter 7
The Two-handed Mouth

Some people feel very strongly about certain issues. Raise the topic of capitalism, for example, and they will have a long list on what is wrong with it. They appear to know exactly where they stand on the issue, and they will let you know in no uncertain terms. In effect, while some might feel that capitalism is the best economic system, others might feel that capitalism is a failure and would present dozens of reasons to support this view.

You, on the other hand, may think that capitalism has its merits and demerits, but you do not feel the need to get angry about the topic one way or the other. Unlike those who cannot see any good in the opinions of their opponents, you, not having a passion for one side or the other, might be able to see the arguments on both sides fairly clearly.

In your conclusion, you need not choose one side or the other. You may wonder, however, if the two sides wouldn't be better off listening a bit more closely to what their opponents have to say. In other words, you need not always take sides in an argument. You can be the voice of objectivity, looking at both sides without bias.

Now, how do you write an essay on a topic on which you do not have strong feelings? More importantly, how do you begin?

Paragraph 1 (Introduction)   Background/General statement(s) on the issue (including definition):

> *Capitalism has been one of the greatest forces in history: the idea that the means of production and distribution ought to rest in private hands, rather than be centrally controlled by the government, has fuelled the success of countries such as the United States and the United Kingdom, allowing these countries to have far more influence and power than one might expect.*

Thesis statement identifying the two opposing strands of thought on capitalism:

> *While some people continue to promote capitalism as the key to economic development everywhere, capitalism's opponents point out that this economic system creates a dangerous gap between the haves and have-nots.*

This thesis statement provides a general idea of what the two opposing sides of the issue are. To make each side of the issue clear you could profit from providing concrete examples. These need not represent your personal views. On both sides of the issue, you can present the views of the supporters or opponents. While you do not have to personally support one side or the other you have to show that you have reflected or thought about the issues carefully.

Your conclusion may simply be that each side makes some good points. If so, however, highlight those points and show how beneficial they are or could be. By the same token, if both sides have some flaws you might want to point them out. Your reflection and thoughts on the ideas presented by the two sides could help the reader gain a deeper insight into the issue under question.

The important point is not just to present ideas on both sides and say goodbye to the reader! Show that you have thought about the issues as well. If possible, offer some advice, suggestions, or raise some points for the reader to consider in connection with the topic in question.

Paragraph 2 could be devoted to discussing the views of those who support capitalism.

> *Supporters of capitalism see this economic system as the cure for the ills of the world such as poverty. They believe that by focusing on individual rights, a capitalist society offers individuals with creativity, energy, and organizational skill an opportunity to contribute to the development of the society. For example, in the United States, the capitalist system allowed people such as Andrew Carnegie to build railroads and for Henry Ford to make affordable cars for America and the rest of the world. Bill Gates is a more recent example of what an individual with good ideas can achieve in a capitalist system. But it is not just individuals who prosper under capitalism. The country as a whole prospers, thus providing the best opportunity for all members of a society to share in the wealth of their collective talents, energy, and effective use of capital.*

Paragraph 3 could be devoted to discussing the views of those who oppose capitalism.

> *Those who speak against capitalism see it as one of the most dangerous economic systems. Capitalism, according to these detractors, is simply a matter of "exploitation of man by man," that is, rich people stealing from the poor! Capitalism provides a legal means by which one human being can enslave another.*
>
> *Under capitalism, the owner of a company is the ultimate winner. He might push his workers to the limit and watch them lose life and limb and still not care as long as they are making his profits grow. Though communism, which was supposed to be an alternative to capitalism, has failed in many parts of the world, those who equate capitalism with evil do not see the failure of communism as meaning that capitalism is any better. Rather, they see capitalism as a runaway train that will kill and hurt thousands, even millions of people the world over, unless it is brought under control – and the sooner, the better.*

Paragraph 4 could be devoted to your own attempt to sort out whether one view is better than the other.

> *There is no question that out of capitalism the world has seen some incredibly good developments. Individuals and private companies that have sought to profit from ideas and investment of capital under the capitalist system have given us some fantastic products that have made life easier for all of us. When people know that investing their time and energy will be rewarded in the marketplace they are willing to take the necessary risks to bring their ideas to fruition. By contrast, in*

a communist system, where the government prefers to keep a strong lid on individual creativity and passions, there is much less prosperity. A careful look at capitalist societies reveals, however, that while there can be many winners, some can also lose out, missing out completely on partaking of the profits and benefits in their society. In the United States, for instance, one of the greatest capitalist nations in the world, with thousands of millionaires, there are more than 30 million people living below the poverty line and a good number of these people do not even have roofs over their heads.

Paragraph 5 could be devoted to a conclusion that invites the reader to make his or her own decision regarding the merits or demerits of capitalism.

It is unlikely that a die-hard capitalist will easily stray away from his or her beliefs. Likewise someone who sees capitalism as evil may not easily change such beliefs. It may be that the truth about capitalism lies somewhere between two extreme images of capitalism. In other words, having unchecked capitalism might highly favor some people, the millionaires, and leave many others unable to put a roof over their heads because of low wages. If the government would let the capitalist system continue to succeeed, but use some of the tax funds collected from prosperous businesses and individuals to help the poor, capitalism might not get such a bad name. One has only to visit Singapore to see that it is possible to marry capitalism with social responsibility.

Assignment 7

1. Assuming you do not have any strong passions one way or the other regarding the issue of abortion, write a 5-paragraph essay about whether abortion should be allowed in the society in which you live. [Please remember that there are arguments on both sides — the so-called Pro Life and Pro Choice factions.]

2. Alternatively, you can choose any other topic that has two strong sides and write your essay on it.

Chapter 8
The Narrative Essay

To narrate means to tell a story. One of the main features of narration is that it follows chronological order, that is, time order. So you tell the reader what happened in time sequence. First, A happened, then B happened, followed by C. This helps avoid confusion for the reader.

The thesis statement in a narrative essay will present the main point of the narration. This may be a lesson learned or an important message that you want to convey. Perhaps, you are telling the story to show that honesty is important or that you enjoyed your visit to the Canary Islands, Spain. Whatever the main point of your narration is, it is a good idea to state it in the introduction and then tell a story that supports this main point. Here is an example of a straight narrative:

> *Yesterday, I woke up at 5 am. Why was I up so early? Well, I needed to complete a work project that I had left untouched for six weeks. After I finished the report, I took a quick shower and dashed out of the house at 7:10, which gave me just enough time to catch the 7:20 train to Orchard Station.*

> *My morning at work started rather badly. The boss seemed to be in a foul mood – as usual, and she gave me an earful about the errors in the report I had given her two weeks earlier Naturally, I apologized, and as expected, she dismissed me with a wave of her hand. I could not wait for lunch. As soon as I heard the chime of the clock at noon I rushed out.*

I phoned one of my colleagues, Mr. Cheong, who joined me for lunch at the food court at Paradiz Centre. Both of us ordered Nasi Goreng and cleaned our plates in ten minutes flat. That left us a lot of time to chat and nurse our glasses of ice tea.

Getting back to the office at 1 o'clock, I found out that my in-box tray was overflowing with projects. I was informed that Ms Li, who shares my work cubicle, had been fired during the lunch hour via a text message from the boss. It was clear from the pile in my in-box that I was now in charge of Ms Li's work, in addition to my own. I worked all afternoon trying to cut the mountain of work down to size. By 4 pm I was beginning to feel the strain. And that is just when the boss returned. She seemed shocked to see me, and especially, with so much work in my in-box. "Didn't you get my text message?" She blurted out. My heart skipped a beat. And then she added: "Never mind. Keep on working. We cannot afford to lose anyone, even terrible workers like you."

The above narration may not carry a message of international significance, but our main character may get to keep his job because the boss is at the end of her rope and resigns herself to keeping a worker she had meant to fire earlier. There are all kinds of narrative essays: some might carry a serious message while others might simply aim to amuse the reader. Whatever you do, try not to bore your reader.

Structure of a story

- Climax (it seems that the main character is at the most dangerous point in the story / the big fight)

- Complication 2 (=event 2)
  - something else happens to make things even more precarious

- Resolution/Denouement (A solution is found; the worst does not happen)

- Complication 1 (=event 1)
  - problem gets worse

- Conflict : main character has a problem
  ex) being bullied? no money? feeling of laziness?

- Start : Introduce main character

the end

Introduction to a Narrative Essay

In a narrative essay, the introduction should carry the main point of the story. As you can see from the above, most stories involve some conflict. While this could be a conflict between or among people, it may also be a person fighting against the elements or even an internal battle. The story progresses through a series of challenges until it gets to the climax, the moment of greatest tension. And then, the issue is somehow resolved.

Model Narrative 1

Learning to speak Japanese

Japanese had always sounded like a difficult language to learn but its "strange-looking" characters and the sound of the words intrigued me. When I found myself on a visit to Japan three years ago, I marveled at non-Japanese who felt so at ease conversing with the Japanese (in Japanese!) and wondered if I too would be able to do so in the future. Though I secretly longed to speak Japanese and to understand the sea of voices around me the possibility seemed remote.

After living in Japan for three months I was no closer to responding to even the simplest of expressions. I relied tremendously on a Brazilian friend who relished speaking Japanese and showing off his skills at every opportunity. At those times when I found myself alone in a shop or at a train station I felt totally at a loss. I resolved to remedy the situation by enrolling in a Japanese language course.

On my first day in school, I expected the teacher to begin with some English explanations. No such luck. The class comprised English, Korean, Chinese, and Bahasa Indonesia speakers. From the get-go we were supposed to communicate in Japanese. The first few lessons were easy enough as the teacher pointed to various objects and indicated their Japanese names. Soon enough I learned the Japanese names of half a dozen objects.

Learning to write was another matter altogether. The Japanese hiragana and katakana are not all that difficult to learn, and yet, I found myself putting it off for weeks. Eventually, I decided to start studying seriously, as I realized that I was in danger of being at the bottom of the class. Within a matter of months, some of my classmates had begun to make long-winded sentences in Japanese. I could only look at them in shock at how well they spoke.

The Japanese course was not exactly cheap; unable to join in the conversations of my fellow classmates, I began to think that I was throwing good money away.

Six months passed.

One day, as I got on the train, I noticed one of my schoolmates, a tall, slender Korean girl, standing next to me. As I stole glances at her she turned her gaze towards me and asked, Doko ni ikun desu ka? My mind raced a mile a minute...but in less than a minute I was able to respond that I was going to Koiwa station. Her face lit up. She was going to the same station.

She seemed to be in a mood for conversation or maybe she had taken a secret shine to me. Whatever it was, there was no escape for me. I could not speak Korean and she could not speak

English. She asked me another question. And another.
The train lurched from time to time but I stood my ground.
By the time we got to Koiwa, fifty minutes had passed and we had been conversing amiably all along. Then it dawned on me: I too could speak Japanese. Between the station and my home, my feet never touched the ground!

Points to consider: Time & Setting of Story

You tell a story by explaining what happened. A story is easier to follow if you start from the beginning, and give the reader an idea of when the events might have occurred. Did the events happen yesterday? Or did they happen several years ago? Such information can be very useful to the reader. It provides perspective. It makes a difference whether something happened yesterday or a decade ago. It would also be important to identify early on who the main character is. That is, who is the story about? This is the main character, also called protagonist.

Put Yourself in Someone Else's Shoes...Sometimes

If you are telling a story about yourself and your funny encounters in a foreign land, you are the main character and you are also the narrator. Sometimes, however, you have to put yourself in someone else's shoes.

For example, you may write a story in which the narrator is a dog.

"When my master, Wing Wang Wong gave me a bone this morning, I could not help but chuckle. There was no meat on the bone. I wondered if we were headed for the poorhouse."

Sample time sequence notes
Follow chronological order/time order

5:07	Woke up
6:30 a.m.	Had a shower
10-15 minutes later	Heard a noise in the kitchen/came out of the bathroom
7:00	Saw a monkey sitting on the stove

Rushed out onto the street
Knocked on a neighbor's door
Neighbor refused to let me in; neighbor called police

5 minutes later	The police arrived/pushed me into their van
	After I explained what had happened, police called animal control
10 minutes later	Animal control officers entered the house and coaxed the monkey out with a banana

Time sequence is important but this does not mean you should focus too intently on it. In the above the time has been left out in some cases. Events at this point were happening in rapid succession, so you don't have to tell the reader that they were occurring seconds or minutes apart. Trust the reader's intelligence.

Also, though following a strict chronological order is a good idea, there is no law that says you should never veer from this format. Remember that, in some cases, the writer reveals the conclusion and goes back to the beginning of the story to let the reader understand how events unfolded to reach that particular outcome.

Break your story down into mini-episodes. If you want the reader to enjoy reading your story try to picture the events in your mind, and write it in such a way that the reader can similarly see mental images as he or she reads your words.

While most narrative stories make an important point, remember that some stories are told just for fun.

Believability

Did you really wake up at 5:07 a.m.? How did you know? Did you check the clock? The reader might wonder about such exactness, so you might want to explain how it is that you know exactly what time you woke up. Think about how you tell stories to your friends. Apply some of those same techniques to your writing.

Model Narrative 2

Those Honest Japanese!

One day, after Japanese language classes, I was in a rush to go meet a friend. At the train station I put a ten thousand yen bill into the ticket machine and quickly grabbed the ticket that popped out. I hurried through the turnstile to catch my train.

I did not have to wait long, but as soon as I entered the train and the door slid shut, I realized that I had not waited long enough for my change from the 10,000-yen to come out of the ticket machine. My friend could wait. As soon as the train arrived at the next stop, I dashed out and went to the opposite platform.

I needed to get back to where I had purchased the ticket in the off chance that no one had gone to the ticket machine after me. Fat chance in a city of 10 million!

Once at the station where I had left my little fortune, I peered over the turnstiles at the ticket machine. My heart sank when I noticed that there were no bills sticking out that would indicate that 9,000 yen was waiting for me, along with 800 yen in coins in the tray.

I went to the station attendant sitting in his booth and tried to explain to him in halting Japanese that someone might have taken my change. A slight smile passed the attendant's lips as he pulled out a brown envelope from a drawer. "Ki o tsukete," he said, and handed me the envelope with 9,800 yen.

I knew enough Japanese to understand that he was telling me to be careful – next time. Whoever might have come to the ticket machine after me must have called the ticket attendant to scoop up the change for me. Ah!!! Those honest Japanese!

The Introduction and Beyond

As with any other essay, it's a good idea if you can give the reader a preview of the main point in the introduction to your narrative essay.

Introduction including a) General Statement to grab the reader's attention + Thesis statement (Main point) that focuses on key points you want to make

Event 1:	buying the ticket at the train station
Event 2:	realizing I had left my change
Event 3:	returning to check the ticket machine
Event 4:	telling the station attendant about my loss
Event 5:	getting my money back with a warning

Conclusion:	Lessons learned/Point of the story

If this were a five-part essay I could have opened the narration with the following introduction.

> *One has to read only a few pages of almost any daily paper to conclude that honesty is virtually extinct. After reading stories of theft, rape, murder, and various forms of lawlessness one could almost be excused for thinking that there is no one left to trust. An experience I had in Japan two years ago, however, has left me with a feeling that while there are indeed many bad people in our midst there are also people (in Japan, and perhaps elsewhere) for whom honesty still means a lot.*

The conclusion in a narrative essay need not be too long.

Action verbs

Action verbs lend excitement to your narrative writing because they create powerful images in the reader's mind.

If you say that John beat Peter, there is no real image - it's a bit boring, wouldn't you say? What about the following?

> *John huffed and puffed in Peter's face. Peter pushed him away and that is when John grabbed his opponent's hair. John repeatedly yanked the younger boy's hair. As Peter screamed, John pummeled him in the chest, kneeing him in the stomach for good measure.*

There is a lot of action here (but don't try any of this at home or anywhere else for that matter!), which puts the reader at the centre of the action...and all because of the use of action verbs. In this regard, your thesaurus may come in really handy.

The Thesaurus - Choosing the Right Word

It is common for us to talk about someone walking up to us or talk about someone walking somewhere. Did the person simply walk? Or is there another word that describes the action better? Did the person stride, pace, amble, trot?

All of these action words evoke a different picture in the mind of the reader. Or when we talk about calling someone, it sounds so bland. Did we yell, bellow, bawl, whisper, shout, summon, or hail?

You can use a thesaurus to help you get the perfect word for what you want to say. In your first draft, you can plop down any word that comes to mind. But, good writing is often a matter of editing and rewriting. So, in your review, think more carefully about which words need to be changed in order to more pointedly express your true meaning.

Action Verbs Galore

Here are some more action verbs, but this should just be the starting point. From now on, become a student of action verbs. They can help you tell stories that will thrill your readers.

Kick

Yell

Leap

Hop

Shove

Yank (Really, don't try this at home!)

Shatter

Other action verbs

Trip	Scribble
Giggle	Jump
Explode	Scream
Sneeze	Sprint
Guzzle	Surge

Of course, other simple verbs such as write, learn, and do, connote action but you may be able to find other action verbs that match much more closely the thought you want to convey. Don't be boring. That's the point.

Good narratives have a point;

they bring to life a moral, lesson, or idea.

– Susan Fawcett, Writer

Find 4 action verbs not mentioned above. Use each to form a sentence.

1. _____

_____

2. _____

_____

3. _____

_____

4. _____

_____

Planning a Narrative essay: Telling a Story

Point of the story:

Protagonist:
(main character)

Antagonist:
(person or circumstance that makes life hard for the main character)

Conflict:
If a bully is making Kareem's life hell in school, you have the beginning of a conflict. How can Kareem deal with this problem?

Note that the conflict can also be something within the main character -- laziness? clumsiness? What could be holding the main character back?

To tell a good story it would be a good idea if things got worse before they got better.

Plot:

Event 1: (what happened?):

Event 2: (then what happened after that?)

Event 3: (what happened further?)

Event 4: climax (the most challenging part of the story/ big problem)

Resolution: the conflicts in the story are resolved

Some words to indicate time order in a narrative essay

First	Before	Later
Next	During	Moments later
Then	After	Finally
Having done that	Suddenly	Immediately after that
Soon	A while later	After a while

Show, don't tell

One of the keys to effective writing is to "show," rather than tell. This can be effective in getting your reader to really "see" what you are writing about. If you tell your reader that a place is dirty or clean or that someone is happy, angry, or sad you rob the reader of the opportunity to come to conclusions herself. Why not show the reader the character's actions or expressions and let the reader decide how the character may be feeling. The key is to make your description so vivid and so clear that the reader can figure out for herself whether the character in question is:

If you can make a reader tell clearly that a character is in a particular emotional, physical, spiritual, or financial state without directly giving the reader such information you are on track. At the end of the following piece, you can decide for yourself whether the character is happy, sad, disappointed or gripped by some other emotion.

Model: Show, Don't Tell

Tracy stroked the mulberry bush and kept her eyes trained on the boarding school gate. Parent after parent said goodbye to some of her schoolmates. Hugs and kisses. Hugs and kisses. Tracy tightened her hold on a mulberry tree branch as one mother squeezed her son in her arms. As the boy waved at her mother, a tear drop fell at the back of Tracy's hand. She quickly brushed it away, but before she turned toward the dormitory, a river of tears flowed down her cheeks.

In order to get good at showing rather than telling, you can imagine being far enough from the character that you cannot hear what he or she says. You can only observe the character's actions, from which, of course, you make judgments. If you are far away enough, but can see someone burying his head in his hands, or banging his head against a wall, wouldn't that tell you something? You may not always make the right judgment as to what is happening, but give the reader a chance to figure things out.

If you've done your job of 'showing' well enough, you can be sure that the reader will not be confused about the emotions being displayed through the character's actions. Consider another example:

> **Model: Show, Don't Tell**
> *The man stretched out his hand to stroke the lady's arm. Bam! The man doubled back as the woman's open palm connected with his jaw. She dove forward and snatched the wallet from the man's breast pocket. His knees buckled, and his back touched the ground. The man tried to stand up, but the woman pushed him down, and pinned him on the floor. From every direction, onlookers streamed towards this noonday spectacle.*

Is this couple having a little fun or serious trouble?

And yet another:

> *As Mayte opened the box, her eyes widened. She stared at the contents of the package and her face lit up. She clasped her hands as if in prayer and grabbed a framed picture on her table. She hugged the picture of her boyfriend long and hard.*

Revealing character

No one likes to read about a boring character. Readers are likely to get drawn into a character if they can identify with the character. It is no accident that children like to read about the antics of other children. You've probably heard of Harry Potter by now!

More than getting the age of your main character right, it helps if the character has some special trait that the reader finds attractive. The character may be intense, humorless, funny, or overly serious. Whatever, it may be, show the character to be more than just a cardboard figure, a flat daddy. Give the character a personality.

You can reveal character through a number of ways, including:
    a) action
    b) dialogue
    c) what others think about the character
    d) character's reaction to his or her surroundings
    e) what the character thinks of himself or herself
    f) setting

a) **Action**

Jojo leaped over the car, kicking and screaming all the while. When someone grabbed his wrist, he tore himself away, sending the poor soul tumbling like a rag doll on the gravel road.

Would you want to get into a little altercation with Jojo?

b) **Dialogue**

Bindy and Bandy stood in the forest clearing. In the distance, the mane of a lion glistened in the hot sun. Bindy stepped back. "We have to get back into the cave at once." Bandy took a step forward and did a little dance, singing, "Oh la la, we have a big dinner tonight!"

Who is brave? Who is scared? You be the judge.

c) **What others think about the character**

People who knew James Brown said he was the kind of guy who would give his friends the shirt off his back. Though he insisted that people call him Mr Brown, most said they would gladly do so.

d) **Character's reaction to his or her surroundings**

Everything in the house gleamed. Some of the paintings that adorned the walls were so lifelike you thought the figures would just step out and say hello. Peter walked briskly across the living room, with eyes trained straight ahead; he fell into the arms of his new girlfriend's father, and hugged him tight.

Is Peter nervous or comfortable in these surroundings?

e) **What the character thinks of himself or herself**

"Yo, I'm the biggest, baddest, winningest coach on the planet and don't you ever forget it. My boys are going to thrash you guys tonight, feel me?"

f) **Setting**

Trees stood like mountains on either side of the road. There was a scent of freshness in the air. Flowers, with yellows dancing in between reds and purples, dazzled the eyes. When I pressed the bell at the gate, a woman dressed like a Beefeater came over. "Miss Warble will presently be with you," she said.

Assignment 8

A. "Show, don't tell" Exercise (Choose 3)

Write a passage that shows that your main character is:

1) happy	6) wealthy
2) angry	7) nervous
3) depressed	8) jealous
4) excited	9) confused
5) poor	10) hopeless

B. Write a narrative essay using your own topic. If you are really stuck for something to write about, you may choose from one of the following topics:

An unforgettable day	A day I'd rather forget
The trip of a lifetime	A visit to grandma
Doing good and doing well	Trapped
A leader is born	Never say never
A new friend	Not just any walk
The rescue	Fire!
The great cookout	A happy coincidence
My 15 minutes of fame	Wrestling with an alligator
Who says animals can't think?	An encounter with greatness
A big disappointment	Looking fear in the eye
A bold move	Extreme shopping
When courage was my middle name	Pure joy
A sinking ship	In search of...

Chapter 9
The Definition Essay

If you define a word or term, you explain clearly what that word or term means. Dictionaries give definitions of words but a definition essay goes beyond the dictionary definition by providing examples that help to clarify the meaning. The starting point, however, is a basic definition similar to one you might find in a dictionary. If you start with a dictionary definition, be sure to note which dictionary it was. For example,

"According to Webster's New Collegiate Dictionary, thespian means ..."

If you do not have access to a dictionary, as might be the case when you are taking an English test, then, you have to create your own basic definition of the word or term as best you can, and expand upon it through the use of various examples.

One of the simplest ways to define a word is to use its synonym or a word that is roughly equivalent in meaning. For example, "to participate means to join" may not win you a Pulitzer Prize, but it can be the first step towards explaining what participation means to you.

Definition through use of a synonym
The starting point is to give a simple definition and then later on expand the definition through examples.

- To participate means to join.
- Courage means to be brave.
- Enthusiasm is excitement.

One of the simplest ways to make the meaning of a word clear is to use a synonym that is much better known. For example, someone asks you the meaning of "obvious." You can say, if something is "obvious," it means it is "clear." It is easy to see or understand.

Similarly, the meaning of "glad" is "happy." Most people understand the meaning of happy, so if they do not know the meaning of "glad," you can indicate that if they understand "happy," then they pretty much understand "glad." Of course, in many cases, there might be slight differences in meaning. In such cases, provide further explanation, or highlight what the differences are.

For example, you can say that "ecstasy" means "joy" or "excitement," but that may not be enough. Ecstasy calls to mind an image of great joy or great excitement.

In a definition essay you attempt to explain a word in many different ways so that its meaning becomes crystal clear to the reader. The more words you have learned the easier it will be for you to come up with a suitable synonym when you most need it. This is why it is a good idea to have a thesaurus on hand at all times.

Recommendations
1) Roget's Thesaurus (Will help you broaden your knowledge of words and their synonyms and antonyms)
2) www.merriamwebster.com (Has both dictionary and thesaurus)

Definition through class

You can define a word by putting it in a class and then showing what makes it different from other things in the same class.

WORD	CLASS	WHAT MAKES IT DIFFERENT
A dictatorship	is a government	in which one person forces his will on others.
An orphan	is a child	whose parents are no longer alive.
Democracy	is government	of the people, by the people, for the people.
A professor	is a teacher	in a university or college.
Monopoly	is control of a market	by one company.
A doctor	is a person	who helps sick people.

Definition by Negation

When you use definition by negation, you say what something is not. You try to eliminate confusion from the minds of your readers by letting them know that they may be carrying the wrong idea about the word or term in question.

For example,

- *Being a good parent does not mean buying lots of toys for your children, but spending time with them.*

- *A university is not a place where students can guzzle large quantities of beer, but a place where they can extend the boundaries of their knowledge.*

- *Freedom isn't the right to punch people in the nose; it is an opportunity to express yourself, while respecting others' boundaries.*

As with other essays, a definition essay can have a thesis statement, which can be embodied in the definition by negation, the definition by class, or by making a particularly important point regarding your understanding of the word.

Let's say your topic is Procrastination.

Procrastination is the habit of delaying endlessly when one has to do something that clearly needs to be done. Many people will freely admit that, at times, they procrastinate. In fact, procrastination is generally considered a bad thing, a killer of success and a habit that people who want to go places will do better to avoid. Although procrastination is considered bad there are times when procrastination can actually be useful.

You would then go on to outline how it is that procrastination can be useful.

IFONI to the rescue! Do you remember IFONI? **Individual**, **Family**, **Organization**, **Nation**, and **International**?

You can, for instance, provide an example in the life of an ***Individual*** and how procrastination helped save the day.

> *When Joji heard that one of her classmates, Nolly, was spreading rumors about her on the Internet, she had a sudden urge to rush to her house and punch the foolishness out of her. She had just returned from a workshop in which the dangers of procrastination had been explained. If she waited any longer, the rumors might spread even further and her reputation would be completely ruined. Joji could not eat that evening. She could only think of the fun that people were going to make of her come next Monday. She decided that, for once at least, she would procrastinate. When she went to class on Monday, she was expecting strange looks from her classmates but everyone was nice as usual. Still, she could not resist finding out where Nolly was and at least, giving her a dirty look. When she asked Laila if she had seen Nolly, imagine her surprise. "Oh my God, so you haven't heard? Nolly had an accident last Friday!*

In this example, you show that procrastination was a "good" thing, not a bad thing for Joji. Imagine if she had gone to Nolly's house to fight, only to hear that she was actually in the hospital.

You can also give an example of how a company (***Organization***) that procrastinated might have benefited in the end, and perhaps, how a family that procrastinated got some form of benefit. This is not to say that procrastination is always good but you are simply helping the reader to appreciate another side of the issue of procrastination, that while in general it might be bad, there are times when it can be a virtue.

Don't be afraid to think along fresh lines; don't be too predictable as a writer. Not a few readers relish the turn of mind of a writer who can delight them with a surprise.

Here's another example: Let's say your topic is Participation.

Par. 1 Intro.   Main point: Participation is not just joining a group but being active in advancing the agenda of the group.

Par. 2 Example 1:   Family (contribution to a family picnic preparations)

Par. 3 Example 2:   Organization (community involvement through volunteering at school, church, etc.)

Par. 4 Example 3:   International (participation in efforts across the world to ease poverty, care for orphans, etc.)

Par. 5 Conclusion: Offer your final thoughts on the issue

Literal versus Metaphorical meaning

You can draw a distinction between the literal meaning of a word and its metaphorical meaning. For example, if your topic is something as mundane as Tiger, you can talk first of all about the tiger, which is a type of big cat found in Africa and Asia. This represents the literal meaning of tiger, that is, a real animal.

After talking about some issues relating to the tiger, such as its power and agility, you can talk about people who reflect these characteristics. For example, if someone says that his girlfriend is a tiger, it may mean that the girlfriend is fierce and that you probably don't want to cross her. This, of course, is merely metaphorical, an image.

On the other hand, Tiger Woods is a golfer who embodies the positive spirit of a tiger, which is fearless fighting and complete confidence in the face of challenge and danger.

Many words in English can be considered both from the literal point of view and the metaphorical.

Consider the following in terms from the literal and metaphorical or figurative perspective:

Word: Snake

Literal	**Metaphorical**
Type of animal	Cunning/dangerous

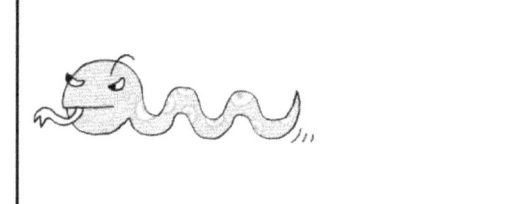 

Word: Rose

Literal	**Metaphorical/Symbolic**
Type of flower	Beauty

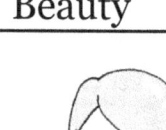 

Word: Tree

Literal	**Metaphorical/Symbolic**
Plant	Stable/Offers protection

Word: Red

Literal	**Metaphorical/Symbolic**
Color	Danger/Prosperity (depending on the culture)

The point here is that you should try to think in a multifaceted way, and not limit yourself to one definition or perception about the topic. It is interesting, for example, that Red, in the West symbolizes danger, but in Chinese culture, it is seen as a symbol of success and power.

Possible outline on the topic of Participation

Paragraph 1   Introduction: General Statement(s) + Thesis statement (Participation is not just joining a group but being active in advancing the agenda of the group)

Paragraph 2   Topic sentence + Example using *Family*

Paragraph 3   Topic sentence + Example using *Organization* (Community project)

Paragraph 4   Topic sentence + Example using *International*

Paragraph 5   Conclusion

Assignment 9:

Write a definition essay on one of the following topics:

A bosom friend	Cool	Loser
Love	Being mobile	Keener
Winning	Trade	Geek
Mistake	Scam	Courage
Growth	A pet	Contentment
Fear	Drug abuse	Disaster
Freedom	A good friend	Enthusiasm
Fraternity	Excuses	Awareness
Leadership	Brother	Family

Chapter 10
The Illustration/Expository Essay

In the classroom or in our daily interactions we are often called upon to explain ourselves or to listen to others explain things. When we listen to the radio or watch television we might hear an expert explain something of topical interest: why the Internet is growing so rapidly, why the U.S. government failed to assist Hurricane Katrina victims, or a new phenomenon such as online learning. Good examples are the key to successful explanation.

Still, do not forget the value of a good thesis statement.

NOTES -- Topic: Distance Education

Paragraph 1: Introduction: General statements + Thesis statement: ....Distance education is increasingly popular because of (1) the flexibility it allows learners, (2) the entry of top-notch universities into the field, and (3) affordability of online programs.

Paragraph 2: Flexibility
- In the past, learners had to go to school full time/be in the classroom
- Now, use of snail mail or Internet allows interaction between students and instructors
- Tapes, CDs, Internet video, WebBoard, BlackBoard, etc., make knowledge easy to impart

Paragraph 3: Top-notch universities have joined the fray
- Some of the early entrants into distance learning were not well known
- In recent years, Oxford, Harvard, Cambridge, have all joined the online learning revolution
- This has brought respect to online learning

Paragraph 4: Affordability
- So many schools, so many opportunities to learn
- Cost has come down / affordable options exist
- Schools in India, South Africa, etc. may be relatively cheap
- Many skill development courses are available for free: web design, photography, etc.

Paragraph 5: Conclusion

Expository essays: Useful at School and at Work

Illustration essays are very important because, in the university, you will have many opportunities to show your skill whether you are studying psychology or sociology, chemistry or kinesics. In the world of work as well, you may have the challenge of explaining products, projects, or plans.

Transitional expressions you might use in an Illustration Essay

- Consider the following case:
- For example,
- For instance,
- An illustration of this is...
- A case in point is when...

Assignment 10:

Write an illustrative essay. Don't forget to use examples. And as always, remember the WriteBurger and include some nifty ingredients such as similes, metaphors, or alliteration, if possible.

Choose one of the following topics:

1) A teacher I can never forget
2) Lessons learned from failure
3) Podcasting
4) How mobile phones have changed the world
5) Computers
6) One small step for a man
7) A journey of a thousand miles begins with one step (Chinese proverb)
8) It takes a village to raise a child (An African proverb)
9) Fashion

Chapter 11
The Descriptive Essay

When you describe something, you use words like a paintbrush. You want your reader to see images. You want your reader to feel the rush of the experience you are describing or to see a place almost as clearly as you might have seen it. In this regard, it is recommended that you keep the senses in mind: sight, smell, sound, taste, and touch.

When you are describing a place the Six-Finger Writing Hand might come in handy:

Place:

Let's say you went to visit Thailand and you want to write about it. Tell the reader what you did there, what you saw there, what you heard, in terms of sounds; a visit to the desert will acquaint you with sounds that differ from those you might hear on the beach or in the forest.

What did you eat (taste)? Fish or berries? How was it? Delicious? Nothing to write home about? Did it make you sick? What about the smells? Was the air fresh and fragrant? Or was it musty and malodorous? Your reader would like to know. And overall, how did you feel?

Place – room

If you need to give specific details about a place, you can describe it from one point of view. For example, you can describe a room as it appears to someone who has just entered. What do you see straight ahead? When you turn your eye to the left, what do you see? What about to the right? Is there anything that really stands out?

Tiny details could also be useful in helping to reveal more about the character of a room. Is there a thick film of dust on the window sill? What does that tell you about the room?

It may tell you that no one has lived in the room for a while. But what if your best friend has been living there for ten years? Does it tell you that he or she is a neatness freak?

Remember: Show, Don't Tell.

Assignment 11 A:

How would you describe the room featured on the previous page? What do you see straight ahead? To your left? To your right? How tidy is the room? What is at the centre of the room? Is it neat? Is it dank?

Try to link the room to the person who lives there. After all, how did you get to see the inside of this room? Who took you there? When did you go there? Morning, afternoon, or evening?

When your essay includes people, it is far more interesting than describing a sterile place. So, even when your goal is merely to describe a place, it does not hurt to put a person in there and include some information on how the place reflects on the individual. Exercise your imagination.

Assignment 11 B: What about this room below? Can you write about the time when you met your principal, a fellow committee member, or a business associate in this boardroom? Try to make your description so vivid that the reader can picture it.

Speaking of People

Consider how you would describe the parade of humanity on display below. If possible, try to make your descriptions indirect (show, don't tell).

Person:

When you are describing a person you often begin with the most striking thing about the person. If you are walking along the street and you meet someone who is taller than a double-decker bus you are not going to call your friend on the phone and say you have seen a handsome guy! You are going to whisper, "You won't believe it. This guy that I'm looking at here on the street is tall, and I mean, tall...tall as in taller than a double-decker bus. Can you believe it?"

After mentioning the dominant feature, you are probably going to move on to other features that catch your eye, features, that will help provide a fuller picture about the person you are describing.

To make it easier for your reader, you might want to break down your description as follows:

1. **Dominant impression:**   Height – Taller than a double-decker bus

2. **Other features:**   Big, floppy ears?
   Kind, watery eyes?
   Hairstyle?

3. **Clothes**   Crisp, Italian suit –
   must have cost a small fortune

4. **Manner/mannerisms:**   Fast walker? Knock-kneed? Bow-legged?

5. **Interactions with others**   Engaging/outgoing? Aloof/Wall flower?

6. **Feeling about the person**   You liked him?
   You felt you couldn't trust him?

As with most essays, there has to be a reason why you are taking the time to write about this person. Why should the reader care about this person? Is he your new brother-in-law or a debt collector?

Average build

I tried to find something special about Joe, who wore the clothes that every other teenager was wearing that summer. His hair flowed in waves and he had two perfect rings for ears but even these did not help make the poor lad stand out from the crowd. He was neither big nor small, and neither short nor tall.

Barrel-chested

Bobolito came by his barrel-chest the honest way. His father had had an immense chest and his grandfather was a mountain of a man. He freely admitted that his luck with the ladies was in no small measure due to the family heirloom – a chest you could write home about!

Beanpole

Shiggy had long since grown accustomed to the nicknames he had been given in school over the years. Eating beans left a bad taste in his mouth and yet this hatred for beans had nothing to do with his being called beanpole at school. He wondered if this was a mere coincidence or if everything was preordained.

Bow-legged

Jagada's legs drew an almost perfect "O" between them. If he stood with his back to me, I imagined I could drive a minivan through those legs, and come out unscathed.

Button nose

The buttons that passed for a nose on Wimwam's face vibrated ever so lightly. Was he angry or was he excited? I had no training in the reading of nose vibrations.

Bulbous nose

Vanferre's nose glowed, not brightly, mind you, but like a dim bulb that brought a sense of calm to frayed nerves. Vanferre was widely known as a good negotiator, but it was not clear if it was this calming effect of his bulbous nose that did the trick or that he actually possessed the powers of mediation that he claimed to have.

Straight nose

Winston's nose was as straight as the highway and just as long.

Eggshaped

Girlfriend says, "The day I met Dobrowsky was the day I stopped eating eggs. His head was the perfect egg and I could not imagine having eggs for breakfast ever again."

High cheekbones

As the lady made her grand entrance into the pin-sized office, her high-cheek bones told me that she was someone important, or at least, she ought to be. Her off-center mouth, however, made me decide that she must have missed a few opportunities in her life.

Knockkneed

When I saw Bananotty coming in the distance, the drumming of his knees against each other made my own knees weak. I knew I had met the love of my life right there on that solitary beach.

Big beautiful woman/ full figured woman

Sandy wore her curves with ease. She carried her weight with such carefree delight that not a few people wondered how a woman as big as she was could carry herself so well on the dance floor.

Hourglass figure

Ma' Rainey was no spring chicken. She had lost some of the oomph in her steps but her hourglass figure could still command the gawks of a thousand men. No, make that ten-thousand.

Overweight

Fat oozed from every part of Natia's body. She was surprisingly strong for a woman that doctors would die to get their hands on for a little tummy-tucking.

Pear-shaped figure

Lucille looked at her cascading hair in the mirror and cast an admiring glance at the pear-shaped beauty staring back at her. "I'm in good company with Oprah Winfrey," she muttered.

Petite

Lolly Tanaka wondered why she could not get a date. She saw the admiring glances from every direction and wondered why no one had the guts to ask her out. Were they afraid she was underage? Had they never heard of the word petite?

Refrigerator-shaped

When I entered the kitchen I wondered how come my mom had not told me she was going to buy another fridge. And then, I realized that it was my cousin Portobello standing next to the fridge. "Good morning," he said, "I arrived last night; you were asleep."

Roman nose

"Everybody loves a Roman nose," bellowed Turkika. "You are about to fall in love with me!" he said to the bewildered young woman.

Slender

"I envy you so much," said Talitha to her pear-shaped friend. "Nobody loves me for me; they only love me for my slender body. How I envy you so!"

Snub nose

Randy Kerr said, "You take one look at my snub nose and you get it into your head that I'm a hoity-toity brat. You're sorely mistaken. I may have been born into money but all I dream about is helping the unfortunate once I've accumulated a bit of coin in the bank myself. That would be a cinch after I finish my studies at Wharton."

Square-jawed

Winkler's square-jawed good looks were part of the reason Emily had fallen for him. Now that his jaws had begun to creak here and there, one had to wonder if Emily's love would endure.

Stocky

Cocky Lucky was no fool. He drank chicken stock for a stocky frame. "All is fair in love and war," he says, "but I'm willing to fight clean; I'm willing to find fights to keep dear Betty and me in groceries all summer long."

Thin/Skinny

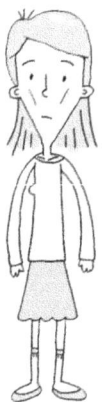

After so many years apart, when I laid eyes on my sister, I could not tell whether she was sick, hungry, or a model.

Triangle head

We debated for hours about whether Peter's head was a scalene triangle, with no sides equal or whether it was isosceles, with two sides equal.

Turned-up nose

Beverly had the perfect turned-up nose for the perfect turned-up face.

Baby-faced

Dr. Paintsill was pushing fifty, and yet once a week, at least, a total stranger would approach him and pinch his ruddy, chubby cheeks. "Story of my life," he says.

Words to Help you Consider Where Things are Positioned

Near to/Next to	Up/Down/Between	Above/Below	Front/Back/Middle
Close/Far	On top of/Beneath	Toward/Away	Left/Right/Center

Preparing to describe

Establish an overall impression at the beginning and let the subsequent paragraphs help prove your point.

Showing, rather than telling about a "Place"

As we neared the cottage Peter touched his nose. Not long after I understood why. I tried to suck in as much oxygen as I could. Peter and I stopped in our tracks. In the distance we could see piles and piles of bodies – carcasses really – of pigs and dogs and cats and deer, some with their throats slit and others in peaceful bloated relief as if they had just lain down for the night and failed to wake up.

What's going on here?

Another example: Showing "Place"

When my hands brushed against the wall it gave up some of its paint. The smell of fresh paint was intoxicating but Joffa, in front, was as eager as I was to lay hands on the treasure in the attic. First there was a creaking sound beneath my feet. When the whole staircase gave way, I felt like a parachutist sailing through a cold wind. As I lay on my back, wondering if I was alive, I saw buckets of blood gush out of Joffa's head. Then I knew that I, at least, was alive.

Assignment 11 C

Choose one of the following and write a 5-paragraph essay (see next page to refresh your memory).

1. My neighborhood
2. A closer look at my pet
3. My favorite tool
4. A visit to ………………………
5. The Perfect Prefect
6. My room
7. My classroom
8. My best friend
9. A doctor I once knew

Alternatively, describe a place or person that made a strong impression upon you, either in your home country or while visiting another place away from home.

PS

For review, you may check out the Classic 5-paragraph essay outline on the next page.

Guaranteed Formula for Writing Success - Everett Ofori

Classic 5-paragraph essay
Video games : good or bad?

- Introduction — General statements (3-5 sentences)

  Thesis statement (1 sentence with 3 points ; show contrast by using "although" or "but")

  > Most people think video games are a waste of time ....
  >
  > Although video games can waste time they can also help children to ①relax, ②develop hand-eye coordination, and ③strengthen friendship bonds.

- Paragraph 1 : Start topic sentence with point 1

  > ① Playing video games can be very relaxing.
  >
  > [Explain with examples ; tell a story, e.g., Louis eases stress after school by playing video games]

- Paragraph 2 : Start topic sentence with point 2

  > ② Frequently playing video games can help develop hand-eye coordination ....
  >
  > [Give examples - surgeons who play video games do better at surgery]

- Paragraph 3 : Start topic sentence with point 3

  > ③ Young people who play the same video games always have something to talk about
  >
  > [Friends play together, shop for new games, discuss games they have played.]

- Conclusion :

  > [Choose a fitting conclusion !]

Chapter 12
The Process Essay

The process essay shows how something is done: how to cook fried rice, how to bathe a baby, how to build a porch.

You can use the introduction to spark interest about why the reader ought to know about "how to do" what you want to talk about.

Thanks to the accident of geography, you may have grown up in a part of the world where you may be familiar with how to do particular things that many others cannot do. For example, a person who has grown up in Japan may know all the proper steps involved in bowing. But how can one explain this so that someone new to the culture can also bow properly. If the steps are explained step by step, it should be possible for someone new to the culture to act like an old pro at bowing.

Many technology products come with instructions on how to use them. Few people can make sense of some of these messages. Obviously, careful thinking is necessary if one is to succeed in presenting a process so that anyone can understand.

There is no question that there is great hunger around the world for people to understand how things are done.

In writing a how-to essay it is a good idea for the writer to declare what the intention of the piece is. For example:

If you follow these directions carefully it will be impossible not to find yourself at the doorstep of Spider Woman!

Indicate what you expect the reader to be able to achieve after reading the paragraph or essay.

Possible outline:

Introduction: General statement(s) + Thesis statement

Step 1:
Step 2:
Step 3:
Step 4:
Step 5:

Conclusion:

Transitional expressions that can assist you with writing a Process Essay

At the start of a piece	In the middle of a process	At the end of a process
At first First Start by... Begin by... Initially At the beginning...	The second step involves... Third.... Then Next Later Before you While As As soon as Having done that Meanwhile During	Finally At last The last thing you do is

Assignment 12

1) From failure to success
2) Organizing a school fair
3) Starting a school club
4) Preparing fried rice
5) How to get to a popular amusement centre
6) How to get to your local library
7) How to choose a college or university
8) How to find a volunteer position
9) How to set up a barbecue
10) How to win friends and influence people (Dale Carnegie)
11) How to persuade your parents to take you to Disneyland

Chapter 13
The Compare and Contrast Essay

Those who study Japanese women, whether as scholars, critics, or admirers, like to draw a distinction between *Yamato Nadeshiko*, the traditional Japanese woman, and *Yamato NadeGucci*, a new type of Japanese woman who delights in shopping for Gucci watches, Ferragamo shoes, and Louis Vuitton bags. They say that where *Yamato Nadeshiko* is moderate and modest, *NadeGucci* is wasteful and showy.

For those less inclined to draw such fine distinctions, what is important is that both *Nadeshiko* and *NadeGucci* spring from the soil of *Yamato* (Japan) and that both are proud of who they are. Finally, both *Nadeshiko* and *NadeGucci* are beautiful, bold, and wise, of course, each in her very own way.

The above is an attempt to draw a distinction between Japanese women, comparing an old ideal with a new exciting incarnation.

Please note that when the similarities between two elements are emphasized, this is considered a Comparison. When the differences are emphasized, this is a Contrast. Often, we want to show both similarities and differences, which is why we talk about Comparing and Contrasting. The list of things you can compare are legion:

Cities: London and New York
Leaders: George Washington and Abraham Lincoln
Theme parks: Disneyland and MGM Theme Park
Friends: Your childhood friend and your current friend
Books:
Movies:
Schools:
Banks:
Holiday experiences:
Products:
Hair salons:
Festivals:

You get the idea.

Compare and Contrast: Places

Let's say you want to compare two places, Hong Kong and Macau. Choose 3 to 5 elements to compare. You can create a table as below to help you organize your material. This can be hand-drawn when you are taking an exam and you do not have access to a computer.

	1) Population	2) Main industries	3) People	4) Leadership
Hong Kong	Small / 6 million	Finance/ Trade	hinese (Cantonese); Formerly controlled by Britain	Chief Executive; successful leadership
Macau	Small / 1 million?	Gambling	Mostly Chinese (Cantonese)/ Formerly controlled by Portugal	Chief Executive -successful leadership

Points of interest

- Both small, though HK bigger of the two
- Both highly successful, one a business centre, the other a playground
- Hong Kongers have a reputation for being hardworking; Macanese? Unsure.
- Both are special administrative regions of China

Paragraph 1: (Introduction)	General statements + thesis statement: Although both Hong Kong and Macau are small, special administrative regions of China, they differ in terms of their colonial background, main industries, and direction for the future.
Paragraph 2:	Highlight the relative sizes of the two territories: quite small compared with Mainland China; Hong Kong is bigger than Macau. Hong Kong colonized by Britain; Macau colonized by Portugal. Both were recently handed over back to China. [Quite a number of similarities here]
Paragraph 3:	Focus on main industries: Hong Kong is a business centre with a strong finance industry and promotes itself as a gateway to China. Macau is known as a playground for the rich; top gambling haven.
Paragraph 4:	Focus on Leadership: Both HK and Macau are run by Chief Executives who are quite popular with the local population and approved by China. Both are forward looking and continually look for ways to improve life for their citizens.
Conclusion:	Prospects for the future are bright for both Hong Kong and Macau even though they rely on different industries for their prosperity.

Another Sample outline:

Paragraph 1:   Introduction

Paragraph 2:   Hong Kong -- location and size
                     Macau – location and size

Paragraph 3:   Hong Kong background and industry
                     Macau background and industry

Paragraph 4:   Hong Kong leadership
                     Macau leadership

Paragraph 5:   Conclusion

Useful transition expressions for making comparisons

- Just as…so
- Similarly
- Like
- Too
- The same
- In the same way
- And; also; in addition to
- As well as
- Each of
- Both, neither

Assignment 13

Choose one of the following and write a compare and contrast essay

1) Shopping in person versus shopping on the Internet

2) Working at home versus working in an office
3) Attending a big university versus attending a small university
4) An optimist and a pessimist
5) Living in Alaska versus living in Alabama
6) Arranged marriages and love matches
7) Your city at night and by day
8) Your friend and your sibling
9) Your favorite activity versus your most dreaded chore
10) A game you currently love to play and one you would like to try in the future

Chapter 14
The Clasification Essay

Classification is grouping things into different categories. It helps readers understand a phenomenon or subject better. Here are some simple classifications:

There are two kinds of people: optimists and pessimists.

There are also men and women; nerds, jocks, geeks, and cheerleaders; type A and type B personalities; and of course, go-getters and couch potatoes.

In the thesis statement of a classification essay, the writer will do well to note what exactly is the focus of the essay and in what way elements are being classified. Once you have identified the categories you want to focus on, the rest may be child's play. Almost!

Optimists and Pessimists

There are over 6 billion people on the planet; they come in various shapes and sizes and complexions, and yet no matter how far you go or how high you go you will discover that at heart there are only two kinds of people in the world: optimists, for whom tomorrow is sure to be a brighter and better day; and pessimists, for whom the worst is just around the corner.

What did we classify? People

Into what groups: Optimists and Pessimists

The essay can then provide some examples of each type.

Sample outline

Paragraph 1: Introduction (Focus on what you are going to classify and why it should be interesting for the reader)

Paragraph 2: Focus on optimists – characteristics; explain with an example or two / tell a story

Paragraph 3: Focus on pessimists – characteristics; explain with an example or two / tell a story

Paragraph 4: Probe deeper: are they equally good or is one better than the other?

Conclusion: Give your reader food for thought

Assignment 14:

Choose one of the following and write a 5-paragraph Classification essay:

1) Students in your school
2) Children in your neighborhood
3) Communication methods
4) Movies
5) Books
6) Music
7) Restaurants in your city
8) Transportation in your country
9) Houses in your country
10) Accommodation for tourists

Chapter 15
The Cause and Effect Essay

Some events are so powerful that they trigger other events. If one event affects another, then the first one is the Cause, and the second, the Effect. If a car hits a bird and the bird dies, the accident is the Cause and the death of the bird is the Effect. You lean against a bookshelf; it falls down. Your leaning against the bookshelf is the cause and the fall of the bookshelf is the effect.

Some causes and effects, however, are not so clear-cut, so you should be careful. Some situations have multiple causes. For example, why are many countries in Asia so successful? Some say the high level of education is the reason; others say the previous support of the United States is a key reason, while for still others, the Confucian tradition in these countries is the most important factor. In this case, there are many possible causes (the three listed earlier) and the effect (success of Asian nations such as Singapore, South Korea, and Japan).

Think through carefully whether there is a connection between the supposed causes and the effects. Do some research in order to understand the phenomenon well. In recent years, there have been many stories about vanishing lakes. The population of the world has also been going up. Is there any connection between these two? What about climate change and vanishing lakes? If you are not sure, do the necessary research.

The late Dr. Martin Luther King Junior was a tireless advocate of civil rights for blacks and other minorities in the United States and around the world. His "I Have a Dream Speech," was a powerful expression of hope for oneness in America and a strong criticism of the country for its hypocrisy. While Dr King did not single-handedly open the way for justice and equality in America, many are willing to acknowledge that the efforts of the civil rights movement as a whole had an effect on the improved conditions of blacks in the United States.

In recent years, the cheap labor in China and the country's skilled labor resources have made it possible for the country to make products that used to be luxuries at prices that many now can afford. How has China's productive capabilities affected patterns of consumption around the world? There may be a cause and effect essay lurking in there.

Celebrity Endorsements: Cause and Effect?

Do celebrity endorsements of products affect the sales of these products? Many companies appear to think so.

In a cause and effect essay, make sure to clarify in the introduction what is the cause and what is the effect. You may also want to note if the connection is strong or weak or indeed if there are other factors that need to be considered. Here's an example:

The Civil Rights Movement (USA)

Paragraph 1: Introduction: General comments plus thesis statement

Paragraph 2: Dr. King made use of logic, reason, and emotion to arouse the conscience of Americans

Paragraph 3: He did not do it alone; there were many powerful organizations behind him

Paragraph 4: Effects of the struggle can be seen today: successful blacks, integration of schools, etc.

Paragraph 5: Conclusion:

Model essay outline:

What accounts for the success of Hong Kong?

Can you identify three reasons why Hong Kong is successful; as with previous essays make sure you have concrete examples, along with figures of speech, topic sentences, and a thesis statement in the introduction.

In a cause and effect essay, make sure that you clearly identify the effect, in this case, the Success of Hong Kong.

Then ask yourself what factors were responsible for the success. Was it the people, the location, the support of China, tourism, or something else. Once you are sure you have identified the causes, some of which may be weak and others strong, you are ready to write.

For example:
A, B, and C --------------------caused------------------------------D (Effect)
HK People, City's Location, and Attractions caused HK's Success (Effect)

For your essay organization, you can have something like the following:

Paragraph 1: Introduction — General statements about HK's success/ Identify people, location and attractions as being responsible for the city's success
Paragraph 2: How Hong Kong's People have contributed to HK's success
Paragraph 3: How the city's Location has contributed to HK's success
Paragraph 4: How special Attractions in the city have contributed to HK's success
Paragraph 5: Conclusion

Model Essay:

Hong Kong is one of the most successful cities in the world in terms of the vibrancy of its economy and the standard of living of its people. Admittedly, there are many things in Hong Kong that fall short, such as the quality of the air. Still, it is impossible to talk about the success of Asian cities without acknowledging that Hong Kong is one of the stars of the so-called Asian Tiger countries and territories. Hong Kong's great success may be attributed to three main factors, namely, the dynamism of its people, the location of the territory, and local attractions that keep tourists coming in from all over the world.

The spirit of Hong Kongers is one of perpetual effort and hope. Even though Hong Kong is such a small territory, it is blessed with people who believe in hard work and effort. From the early days of Hong Kong's history, its people set up factories, built harbors, and struggled to make the territory a gateway to the Orient. Individuals such as Li Ka Shing, Hong Kong's richest person, embody the spirit of Hong Kong and show how effort can translate into success. Even now, Hong Kongers like to say, "No challenge, no success!" or words to that effect. Hong Kong is a veritable beehive of activity. Whether you are walking down Nathan Street where you can see colorful shops selling anything from jewelry and shoes to watches, or lost among the high-rises in the Central district, you can tell that the people of this city stride with purpose and work with determination.

The location of Hong Kong has also been useful in the territory's success. At a time when China was virtually closed to the outside world, Hong Kong was able to take advantage of its proximity to China to act as a go-between for Western countries that wanted to trade with China or have a foothold in the Asian market. Because the people of Hong Kong speak both Chinese and English they were able to trade successfully with Western countries and become a conduit for bringing Western expertise to Asia, *while at the same time selling prized Asian goods to the West. The location of the territory close to other important Asian cities such as Shanghai, Taipei, Singapore, and even Tokyo helped to make it an important hub for business people both for manufacturing and shipping.*

In recent years, tourism has contributed greatly to putting Hong Kong on the map for people who do not care so much about business. For those who are attracted by the beauty of Asia, Hong Kong offers an opportunity to see the Orient in all its splendor, from lush groves and landscapes to man-made attractions such as amusement parks. In particular, tourists never seem to tire of Ocean Park, with its marine animal shows and aquarium, and the Peak, which offers a magnificent view of the city. The city's temples and inexpensive goods also bring in hordes of shoppers from around the world.

Hong Kong's success cannot be linked to only one factor. Without the territory's hardworking people, the city might have continued to be a fishing backwater. Without the city's location close to China and other equally great Asian cities Hong Kong might not have been able to develop itself into a financial and shipping hub that is seen as a key to international trade. And finally, without a full range of activities and attractions to engage tourists the territory might not have enjoyed record numbers of people coming in every year. Recently, given China's full backing of the territory in its economic endeavors there is no question that the success of Hong Kong will continue for a long time to come.

Assignment 15:
Choose one of the following and write a Cause and Effect essay. Plan carefully.

1) TV and its influence on children
2) Pollution
3) Computers and lifestyle
4) Airplanes
5) Fast food
6) Illiteracy
7) Sports
8) Depression
9) Overpopulation
10) Forest fires
11) Global warming
12) Being a couch potato

Chapter 16
The Persuasive Essay

Persuasive essays challenge the writer to present arguments that will help change the thinking of others. There are many occasions in life when we might have to persuade others to our point of view.

Whatever your point of view might be on a subject, it might be that others do not share the same view. Are you able to convince others to come around to your point of view? If you have powerful enough reasons, it may be possible to do so. You may not be able to persuade people to change their minds (lastingly, anyway) by pointing a gun at their heads, but through your arguments you can plant a seed in someone's mind that will blossom in time, possibly translating into a changed opinion or viewpoint.

Often, in order to argue effectively, it is useful to anticipate what arguments opponents of your point of view might have. This helps you to provide counterarguments to these opposing views. If you are able to quash the arguments that go against your own point of view, then you would have opened the way for your reader to possibly accept your views.

Writing a persuasive paper does not mean shooting down every idea you don't agree with. In fact, in order to achieve your goals, you should begin in a way that will draw your reader in and entice him or her to read and then by patient turns change the reader's mind.

If you believe in capital punishment you might not be interested in preaching to others who share a similar view. You do not want to preach to the converted. Rather, you should consider the views of those who oppose capital punishment and then think about whether you have more powerful arguments against those views.

Those who oppose capital punishment might say for example that it is important to respect life and that capital punishment is not effective as a deterrent.

A direct and immediate attack against the opposing position might harden the heart of the reader and make it difficult for you to get your points across. If the opposing side has some good points, acknowledge it. This will make the reader more receptive and consider the writer fair-minded.

Persuasive Essay: Key points to keep in mind
1) Start with common ground
2) Be respectful of those who do not share your opinion
3) Use facts and figures
4) Use emotion where necessary but do not overdo it
5) Introduce opposing arguments and show why they are weak

Assignment 16:
Choose one of the topics below or any other topic of your choice. Make sure that there is a definite point of view and try to persuade the reader to favorably consider your point of view. Don't forget the rule of three, and do not forget to raise opposing points and show why they are not valid.

1) War on terror
2) Corporal punishment
3) Capital punishment
4) Helping the homeless
5) Hip hop music
6) Cosmetic surgery
7) Use of steroids in sports
8) Climate change
9) The ivory trade
10) Child brides

Chapter 17
Getting Better as a Writer

Read as widely as possible, including books and materials that you would normally not want to read. For example, if you do not usually like to play sports or watch sports, read sports magazines anyway. You will learn a lot from the practice.

Signposting

Most readers benefit from getting a sense in your introduction of where you want to take them. This is particularly the case when you are writing articles or scholarly papers. But even fiction can raise enough intrigue at the beginning to make the reader eager to go on a journey of discovery with the writer.

Originality

Many great writers readily admit to being avid readers. This means, then, that over a lifetime, they pick up many ideas and saturate their minds with words and expressions that contribute to making their own minds fertile for creativity. It is quite normal for writers to pay attention to how other writers have achieved certain effects and to aim to do even better. But this is completely different from making it a habit of copying what others have painstakingly written. It is always a sad story when the news breaks that a highly respected writer has been caught using the words of another without attribution. There is a word for it — plagiarism.

Give Credit

When you borrow the words of others, acknowledge it. It does not take much to say, "According to...." to signal that you borrowed some particular words from a particular person.

Please do not fall into the trap of borrowing the words of others and passing them off as your own. People might have gotten away with such behavior a hundred years ago, but in this new era of the Internet, it is one of the fastest ways to cut up your reputation into shreds. Besides, if you want to be a good writer, you should be willing to put in the work, as all notable writers have done.

The Gold Beneath Your Feet

Beginning writers seldom see the gold beneath their feet or the gold in the vaults of their own lives and experience. They are apt to think that the life they have led to date is less exciting than that of the greying former CEO whose yacht is berthed in a marina at Bermuda. They might think that the stuff of their lives is not interesting to anyone. And so, it is not unusual for the farm girl who knows everything about potato mounds and corn husks to attempt to write about the lives of the rich and famous. She fails miserably, of course, because her writing does not have the ring of truth.

But this same farm girl, if she has been observant enough about the life into which she has grown up, could share details of that life and hold millions of people spellbound. Those unfamiliar with the world of farms and pigs and beans would gladly enter into her world — to learn or to be amused.

So do not discard your own experience, or think that your life is not interesting enough. It has been said that there is no boring subject, only boring writers. Find the hidden gold in your life and polish it as best you can.

What's Your Angle?

Take a simple case of city living in a place like Tokyo. The way a Japanese salaryman experiences life in the city, through his long hours of work, long commutes, karaoke nights, and weekend golf, may have some similarities with how a fishmonger in the city experiences it. But if they focused on what was unique to their lives, they could write stories that are different enough but with each charming in its own way. Whereas the salaryman may write from the perspective of the office worker or businessman the fish monger may see the world from a completely different angle, dealing with restaurant owners who want the best fish to land on their cooking table.

Likewise, when you take a family in distress, the same story could be written from the point of view of the father, the wife, the children, the grandparents, or even neighbors. Each perspective is different.

Not surprisingly, one of the most common elements newspaper writers seek is the angle from which to approach a story. Should they write about how one athlete almost always wins or should they focus on the few times when she had lost and how she handled that loss? What's your angle on the story?

If you want to keep getting better as a writer, here are a few other suggestions:

- Write everyday if possible.
- Write down words and phrases you encounter in your reading of newspapers, magazines, fiction, etc., and try to use them in conversation or in your own writing.
- Be a lifelong student of grammar.
- Read books on writing.
- Take a writing workshop or course.

- Sleep with a thesaurus under your pillow.
- Make sure that you have a trusted dictionary within easy reach at all times.
- Expand your vocabulary but take your audience into consideration when choosing words. Often, the simpler, the better.
- Read topnotch newspapers and magazines such as The New York Times, The Washington Post, The Economist, Newsweek, and Time.

- Read biographies to find out how others were able to achieve their goals.
- Read self-help books for motivation.
- Learn public speaking -- in case you become famous!

Extra Practice:
Think, Plan, Write & Revise

Maya Angelou, the American poet and writer, said, "I've learned that people will forget what you said, but they will never forget how you made them feel." Do you agree? What is your view on this statement?

Extra Practice:
Think, Plan, Write & Revise

John Donne, the English poet, wrote: "No man is an island, entire of itself; every man is a piece of the Continent, a part of the whole."

What does the above mean to you? Explain with examples.

Extra Practice:
Think, Plan, Write & Revise

Nigerian novelist, Chimamanda Ngozi Adichie, wrote: "Stories matter. Many stories mantter. Stories have been used to dispossess and to malign, but stories can also be used to empower and to humanize. Stories can break the dignity of people, but stories can also repair that broken dignity."

What does the above mean to you? Explain with examples.

Extra Practice:
Think, Plan, Write & Revise

Anne Frank, the Jewish writer, noted: "Look at how a single candle can both defy and define the darkness." What does the above mean to you? Explain with examples.

Chapter 18
101 More Topics for Writing Practice

1. A person you have always admired and why
2. The National Anthem
3. Use of your leisure time
4. Impact of divorce on young people
5. Items from your culture that others should know about
6. Career goal
7. Describe a laundry room you know
8. Climate change
9. Money matters
10. Homework
11. A proud moment in your life
12. A talented person you know or know of
13. Stress and its effects
14. An animal whose spirit represents the kind of person you are
15. False advertising
16. Censorship
17. Foster homes
18. Students and cell phones
19. Air travel and security
20. Indigenous people
21. Genetically modified food
22. Organ donation
23. Clinical trials
24. Friendship
25. Statistics: A liar's best friend
26. One brave moment
27. Living with hope
28. Sexism
29. Ecotourism

30. Gender equality
31. The death penalty
32. Modeling
33. Charities
34. Plant and animal extinction
35. The good old days
36. A crisis always has two sides: risk and opportunity
37. The United Nations
38. A teacher who had an impact on your life
39. Lying and liars
40. Making choices in life
41. Adoption of children
42. Human migration
43. Risk taking
44. The role of religion in society
45. Protecting the rights of animals
46. Standardized tests
47. Curfews
48. Drinking and driving
49. The impact of music on your life
50. Videogames
51. Teen pregnancy
52. Young people and gangs
53. Vegetariamism
54. Life is what you make it
55. Xenophobia
56. Private prisons
57. Character counts
58. Poetry: What is it good for?
59. Entrepreneurship
60. Violent video games
61. Celebrities
62. Homeschooling
63. Genocide
64. Parents
65. Tobacco
66. Young girls focus too much on makeup
67. Oil spills
68. A journey of a thousand miles begins with one step. (Chinese proverb)
69. My favorite movie
70. The reading road is a road that leads to success
71. Myths and legends

72. Preservation of minority languages
73. Fashion
74. Architecture
75. Mathematics: What is it good for?
76. Art and music programs
77. Acting as a career
78. Learning from failure
79. Museums
80. Favorite dish
81. Bodybuilding
82. Gun control
83. Zoos
84. Space travel
85. The European Union
86. Minimum drinking age (alcohol)
87. Progressive taxation
88. The war on drugs
89. Foreign aid
90. Abortion
91. Famine
92. Overpopulation
93. School uniforms
94. Tattoos
95. A place you would love to live
96. What you would like to invent
97. What you would change about the world if you had the power to do so
98. A life-changing book
99. Second chances
100. Overcoming fear
101. Truancy

About the Author

Everett Ofori holds an MBA from Heriot-Watt University (Scotland, UK) and a Master of Science, Finance, from the College for Financial Planning, Colorado, USA. He teaches Public Speaking, Management, Marketing, and English for Specific Purposes (Business Writing, Medical Writing, Meeting Facilitation, etc.). Everett has helped hundreds of high school and university students around the world to improve their writing and grades. He has also worked extensively with business executives (including those at the C-level).

Everett has worked with clients/students from the following organizations and more:

• Accenture	• Actelion
• Asahi Kasei Medical	• Asahi Soft Drink Research, Moriya
• Astellas	• Barclays
• Becton Dickinson	• Chugai Pharmaceuticals
• Disney	• ExxonMobil
• Fujitsu	• Goldman Sachs
• Gyao (Yahoo Japan)	• Hitachi Design
• IIJ (Internet Initiative Japan)	• Johnson & Johnson (Janssen)
• McKinsey Japan	• Mitsubishi (Shoji)
• Moody's	• National Institute of Land and Infrastructure Management, Tsukuba, Japan (NILIM)
• Orix	• PriceWaterhouseCoopers (PWC)
• Recruit	• Sekizenkai Nursing School, Soga, Kanagawa
• Sumisho	• Summit Agro International
• Sumitomo	• Suntory
• Tokyo International Business College, Asakusabashi, Tokyo	• Yokohama Child Welfare College (Hoiku Fukushi), Higashi Totsuka, Kanagawa

Notes

www.ingramcontent.com/pod-product-compliance
Lightning Source LLC
Chambersburg PA
CBHW081112080526
44587CB00021B/3567